ADVANCE PRAISE

As a longtime fan, I've read a lot on these guys and their music. From *Higher & Higher* to many of the rock-critic website communities. I have all of their albums, including the "Core 7" on vinyl.

The Whitfields have not only covered their history, career and music, but they have gone below the surface to give us what, with all my knowledge about the band, I have to call this book *The Definitive* writing on the Moody Blues.

William Pliska, Seattle

The authors take my understanding of The Moody Blues' romantic and ethereal lyrics to the next level. I discovered more and deeper reasons about why I have found the Moodies' songs so captivating and moving for so many years. I now listen to them with a deeper appreciation and I understand the wisdom of their lyrics and power of their music far better.

They are indeed timeless.

Don Best −longtime listener and fan, Atlanta

Since the 1960's ushered in a wave of cultural change, many of our poets and prophets have been rock musicians. Bob Dylan and the Beatles get most of the credit, but The Moody Blues deserve top billing in this area as well. Timothy Leary may be dead, but not the Moody Blues tune about him and the wisdom that emerged from that era as reflected in the Moodies' countless other songs, which the authors so beautifully describe in a depth that I had not previously considered.

To have Charles and Barbara Whitfield, such expert consciousness explorers themselves, compare the MB's lyrics against other maps of consciousness enhances one's deeper appreciation of their songs. Reading this book has been a pleasant journey of reconnecting to the sounds that moved me back in the 60s and 70s. But now, with an enhanced personal perspective amplified by the authors' psychological and spiritual savvy, I am much better able to plumb the depths of this soul music.

David Lukoff PhD, Professor of psychology
Sophia University, Palo Alto, CA

TIMELESS TROUBADOURS

The Moody Blues'

MUSIC AND MESSAGE

THEIR CREATIVITY AND POETRY
—ROMANTIC, SPIRITUAL, TRANSCENDENT
AND PRACTICAL
FOR HEALING RELATIONSHIPS
WITH SELF, OTHERS AND GOD

CHARLES L WHITFIELD MD
BESTSELLING AUTHOR OF *HEALING THE CHILD WITHIN*
&
BARBARA HARRIS WHITFIELD RT, CMT
AUTHOR OF *SPIRITUAL AWAKENINGS* & *THE NATURAL SOUL*

MHP
muse house press

muse house press

ISBN: 978-1-935827-15-3

Cover design and Interior composition by:
Donald Brennan / Muse House Press / YakRider Media

Key words: music, poetry, consciousness, spirituality, 1960s, relationships, meaning, healing, recovery

Direct requests to: inquiry@MuseHousePress.com

Visit us on the Internet at:
 MoodiesBook.Wordpress.com
 www.MuseHousePress.com
 BarbaraWhitfield.Blogspot.com
Muse House Press and the MHP Logo are imprints of Muse House Press

Attribution for all of the photographs in this book was not possible since many of them are in some cases forty-plus years old and the photos are scattered across the Internet without attribution. However, we have made a best-effort attempt to track down the photo owners and provide credit.

Printed in the United States of America
First printing

Also available in **Kindle**

ON THE COVER

The cover art is from an oil painting that I painted in 2012. I modeled it after both the 16th c. art attributed to Sulamith Wolfing and esp. the British artist Phillip Travers album cover art for the Moody Blues 6th of their seven classic first albums *Every Good Boy Deserves Favour*, released in 1971.* I separated the image of the boy from the man by a small additional space, added rays emanating from the crystal, and there are other small differences. The painting captures one of the Moodies' subjects and themes throughout their creative and storied careers—the power of seeing through the eyes of a child (4th album *To Our Children's Children's Children* 1969). Some have imagined that the boy represents a young King Arthur and the man Merlin. References to Merlin in their music are in other of their songs as reflected in 'Are You Sitting Comfortably' (lyrics by Ray and Justin) from their 1969 3rd album *On the Threshold of a Dream*:

> Ride along the winds of time and see where we have been,
> The glorious age of Camelot, when Guinevere was Queen.
> It all unfolds before your eyes
> As Merlin casts his spell.

The child represents our Real Self, which I have also called the Child Within throughout my other books. The man represents the Higher Self (also called Guardian Angel, Atman, Christ Consciousness).

Charles Whitfield MD & Donald Brennan

* Travers painted all of their classic seven albums' cover art except for that of *Days of Future Past*. which was painted by David Anstey. www.philiptravers.co.uk/index.html See also: en.wikipedia.org/wiki/Merlin & wiki/Arthurian_legend

ACKNOWLEDGEMENTS

The authors thank The Moody Blues co-founders Ray Thomas and Mike Pinder for reading and fact-checking this book. [59, 77] Through their agents [100] we offered Graeme Edge, John Lodge and Justin Hayward this book's first draft for their corrections and comments, and we could not reach them directly.

All lyrics that we reproduce for our interpretation or making meaning are written by The Moody Blues authors and copyrighted by them and/or their appropriate publisher. [43]

DEDICATION

We dedicate this book to the Moodies' countless fans and all spiritual seekers throughout the world who have the awareness to appreciate their poetic, lyric and musical art.

ABOUT THE AUTHORS

Charles and Barbara Whitfield live and practice in Atlanta, Ga. They specialize in assisting adults who were traumatized as children and later in life, and people with addictions. Charles has written several best selling books and has co-authored eight published articles on trauma effects while working at the CDC in Atlanta. Barbara is a consciousness researcher, an author of nine books and is a therapist in private practice with her husband doing group and individual therapy.

TABLE OF CONTENTS

FOREWORD BY MIKE PINDER

It was very interesting to read Charles and Barbara Whitfield's interpretations of our music and message.

They suggest clear and useful ideas and ways for those who are newly exploring our music and for the many who have been on this journey with us from the beginning.

I have always been interested in the broader qualities of music to inform, heal, raise consciousness and uplift. This was often on my mind when I wrote a song or painted the backdrop for others in the band with counter melodies and my mellotron.

In contrast to most observers of our music, I saw how the authors here delve below the surface and give us an enjoyable interpretation of our words and music. They examine essentially their every aspect. Not only do they address our lyrics from a scholarly and poetic perspective, but they offer us some insightful and sometimes surprising interpretations of them beyond what many listeners and fans may consider.

Music has changed our world. It has the potential for reaching within, opening our minds and our hearts to the power of Universal Love. It transforms, strengthens, relaxes, teaches and enlightens us.

The Whitfields realize these truths and give us a strong base from which to experientially understand them. They integrate the many positive messages of our words and music by giving us a clear and constructive map of healing that is on the cutting edge of psychology, consciousness studies and spirituality.

Memories are also closely associated with music. I have always thought that we hang our memories on the shape of sound. With memorable melodies, counter melodies and instrumentation we were able to create soundscapes for many to hang the best memories of their lives.

Those of us who remember the 1960s and beyond will appreciate their attention to the detail of our works and the history of how it all came about.

They show us how the Moodies have expressed, preserved and continue to remind us of the message and wisdom of the 60s by keeping it so alive. And how there was a natural spirituality that still lives in all of us and that is manifested in our descriptions of Love.

Mike Pinder
March 2013

Introduction

They didn't form overnight. The Moody Blues were and remain essentially self-taught as musicians, none claiming any special training beyond piano lessons or school band activities in childhood.

BAND 1

Their beginnings evolved over a ten year gestational period of being first inspired, interested and finally involved in writing, developing, rehearsing and performing their own music, as shown in the **Timeline** in the Appendix on page 136.

Soon, in a phenomenal burst of creativity over a five year period from 1967 through 1972, they made seven hit albums —which we can call their first and *classic* or *core 7*— that contained 68 songs, nearly all of which were impressive.

To our knowledge, no one has chronicled their monumental achievements and insights in one detailed writing. In this book we go beyond that goal. We document, describe and analyze the power of their music, poetry, spiritual psychology and message.

To do this we start with the words of their music: their lyric poetry, conventionally called lyrics. Then in Chapters 2 and 3 we look at their first album and analyze each song of *Days of Future Past*. Then we address the rest of their work according to how we see their music and poetry relate to our levels of consciousness. We believe that their music is not just entertaining, but it is enlivening and healing, which may be a factor in their voluminous sales, radio and internet exposure and consistent fan concert attendance over the last nearly five decades.

Their co-founder and keyboardist, singer and composer Mike Pinder described their evolution as happening in two stages. He called these Band 1 and Band 2. Band 1 did mostly R&B and included members Pinder, Ray Thomas, Graeme Edge, Denny Laine and Clint Warwick. Together over about two years, they first called themselves the M+B 5, named after the Mitchells & Butlers Brewing Co that owned pubs where they had hoped to perform in the pub circuit in Birmingham, but which did not happen. Then they changed their name to the Moody Blues and soon fortunately with Decca Records made their only album as Band 1 called *The Magnificent Moodies*. Their only real hit then was "Go Now."

In June 1966, through what appeared to be a remarkable series of synchronicities, Clint Warwick left the band to be with his wife and children. Four months later in October Denny Laine departed, leaving them without a lead singer and a bass guitarist. John Lodge joined the band in 1966 after Clint left. Justin Hayward was added after October 1966 when Denny left, and that was another of this series of synchronicities.

Still looking for a lead guitarist and singer, Ray and Mike ran into Eric Burdon of The Animals band who gave him a list of names, from which he and Mike found Justin Hayward who had just become free to join them and complete their new band as Band 2. Luckily too, Burdon had just picked another lead guitarist for his group and had not selected Justin. Decades later, Graeme Edge commented on their good fortune: "I'm not sure how it all happened, but we put in our thumb and pulled out a plum!" [54]

BAND 2

Throughout their music as Band 2, which remains active today, the Moodies musically addressed these perennial questions: Who am I? What am I doing here? Where am I going? How can I get any peace? As Douglas Adams wrote in his serious science fiction spoof *Hitchhiker's Guide to the Galaxy*: What is the answer to life, the Universe and everything? [1] Important questions...

Mystics, sages and spiritual seekers have searched for enlightenment, peace and spiritual evolution with a connection to God. We see the Moody Blues as not only spiritual seekers, but serious explorers, co-creators, and cultural creatives who have used their God-given faculties and talents to share with the world their experiences and insights through their clear, haunting, enlivening and spiritually stimulating music—which we describe in some detail throughout this book.

Over the decades they have given us what we see as their remarkable yet simple take on our relationships with our self, others and God. They have done that impeccably through their lyric poetry enfolded in music that is clearly captivating, at times fanciful, and often spiritual—yet real-life-applicable with their exceptional melody and entertaining poetic and inspirational stories. Their music and delivery helps us transcend the ordinary—not only into the imaginal realm, but deep inside our minds, hearts and souls—our very consciousness itself.

Consciousness and Healing

In this book we describe how and why hearing and listening to the Moody Blues music is consciousness raising and healing. We have addressed both consciousness and healing in everyday life—outside of music—throughout our previous books. [86-91]

Over the decades the Moody Blues' inspiring and healing musical work parallels ours in our books and the assistance we have given trauma survivors and spiritual seekers. We explore, address and highlight levels of consciousness—which are essentially the same as levels of healing.

We use our experience listening to the Moodies' music for decades, studying it, and the clear comments and insights of the band and others' who knew or were close to them. Throughout this book we select a few among their songs to illustrate our experience and observations and their own words from their interviews and other sources.

Words alone here will not be enough. We recommend when reading about any of their particular songs here that you also *play those songs*—which we believe will make our comments and your appreciation and enjoyment of their music come more alive. Pull out your Moodies' old vinyl records, CDs, or other stored digital music and *listen while you are reading* this book.

In the universe of music—popular, classical, classic rock, art rock, progressive rock, psychedelic rock, new age, folk and country, the Moody Blues incorporate aspects of all of these except country music. No group has embodied this vast a spectrum of music so successfully and for so long. No group in any genre within this spectrum has generated so many songs so well—and done so at such a high level of consciousness.

Some have called Elvis the "King of Rock 'n Roll" and Michael Jackson the "King of Pop," etc. While some have called the Moody Blues the "Kings of Classic Rock," [76] we would consider adding to that title the "Kings of Higher Consciousness" (i.e., the integration of ordinary consciousness with our higher levels of consciousness, which we describe throughout this book). We see their music and message as having to do with psychological and spiritual growth.

We see it as expanding our reality by assisting us to begin to experience Reality with a "capital R." Recently Barbara wrote about her loving their lyrics on an Internet blog for Near-Death Experiencers and others interested in higher levels of consciousness. We were surprised at their numerous positive comments about their music. Many if not most of that blog's members said that they have followed the Moodies since the 1960s.

We have many choices to appreciate and understand their perspectives and qualities. The Moody Blues have filled our lives with entertainment, love, joy, curiosity about life, spirituality and clear questions about life's real meanings. They've answered some of those questions and with deep responses not connected to any religion, but to an *expansive natural spirituality*.

Our own grand children ages 3 and up share our joy when we play their songs and concert DVDs. We have spent hours with these youngsters who seem to understand on their own level that this is *fun*, *important* and *joyful* music. This reminds us of some of their great pieces such as "Eyes of a Child." And when 4—year—old Lily gets in the car, she often says, "Put on 'Say it with Love!'"

Charles L Whitfield MD
Barbara H Whitfield RT, CMT
Atlanta. GA

In the Amsterdam Airport 1971 [98]

1 THEIR LYRICS AS POETRY

We believe that the Moodies' poetry as embodied in their lyrics and wrapped in their mood-lifting music is a major factor in their continued popularity over the decades. With their message of openness, spirituality and love, we see their poetry as reminiscent of and fitting in with that of the great romantic poets of the late 1700s and early 1800s. Their lyric poems also are to a degree compatible with that of the best of the troubadours from the middle ages and the mystical spiritual poetry of all faiths over the millennia. (The ancient term *Lyric* is pertaining to the lyre, and adopted for singing with the Greek classical instrument.)

POETRY AND THE MOODIES

Poetry is the art of expressing thoughts, feelings, ideas, observations, experiences and facts in verse. Compared to ordinary speech, it does so in a style more concentrated, imaginative and powerful. A song is simply poetry put to music. Both sensuous and cerebral, heart and head, poetry and music come from both our conscious and unconscious mind. Coming from their unconscious, most poets do not consciously know all of the subtle meanings they intended for all their words or phrases.

When the five Moodies wrote and composed the 68 pieces for their core 7 albums, they were all young men who were exploring the answers to perennial questions such as: Who am I?, What am I doing here?, Where am I going? and How can I get any peace? In short, What's our life all about?

As they made their music, they had several *factors interacting*, and with success: 1) They were bright and inquisitive people exploring the nature of self, others and God, 2) Their influences from the 1960s' culture and music (which actually went from 1963 to 1974), which included 3) The occasional use of alcohol and other psychoactive drugs, and their sporadic use of psychedelic (mind or soul expanding) drugs, 4) Their superb use of orchestration via the Mellotron (described in Chapter 14 below) and 5) Their own innate individual and group talents and creativity.

Critic fan John McFerrin said, "...the classic Moodies' albums represent a point of view nearly completely devoid of cynicism, jadedness and all of the other attributes that callous over our souls as we age and go through the hard times of life. ... The general attitude of the band had nothing to do with the guts of rock music, which of course is ultimately about getting high, screwing groupies and beating people up. ... The viewpoint of the Moodies, in my mind, is the world as seen through, you guessed it, the eyes of a child. You can call it childish; I call it child*like* .... The world has enough bands describing reality as [they may think] it is; it needs one band describing reality how it arguably *should be* ... ." [46, 87, 90]

This optimism is in part why —over nearly 50 years

—their fans keep listening to their music, attending their concerts, and talking about them so positively in print, [9, 50, 51, 62, 92] online and elsewhere, including our writing about them and your reading this book. Instead of songs about crazy relationships, anger, violence, and other negatives, common from many bands, the Moodies have explored, addressed and described universal questions, truths and wisdom from a more positive and constructive perspective.

UNDERSTANDING AND INTERPRETING IT

Let's look at poetry and ways we can understand it better. Most other writing forms are longer and try to explain something—a scene, a situation, idea, a set of instructions, an experience. Poetry and lyrics *don't explain*. They express. They show. They paint a picture, take a snapshot, and then pull us into it. [93, 94] Their strings of words are usually brief and more concentrated. The poet is often able to tell the truth on a deeper level, able to see patterns and overarching themes. [57]

The poet is exploring their *inner* and *outer life* to try to figure out and understand them better. They usually go into a kind of self-induced trance or altered state of awareness or consciousness to write what comes up for them, briefly and in verse. Poetry is a shorthand and encoded form of creative writing that opens itself to interpretation by us all.

• To better understand and appreciate poetry, consider reading this summary analysis of Robert Frost's classical short poem "Stopping by Woods on a Snowy Evening" *online* at: faculty.gvsu.edu/websterm/Readpoem.htm or do another search for it. We believe that this is an excellent and easy read, and it makes reading the Moody's poetic lyrics overall more understandable. [60]

LEVELS OF LISTENING AND UNDERSTANDING

When we interpret a poem we are explaining one or more ideas, references, allusions, imagery and messages in the poem. A good poem and song can reach us on three levels: the *literal*, *figurative*, and *sonic*.

On the first and **Literal** level, the words tell a small or brief story about something. This little story may at first be mildly or moderately interesting, e.g., in Mike Pinder's 'Have You Heard?' that ends their *OtToaD* album: "Now you know that you are real / Show your friends that you and me / Belong to the same world / Turned on to the same word / Have you heard?... . " Some to many aware listeners may suspect that there probably is *more* to the words, especially when they are enfolded in their glorious and often transcendent music and voices.

At least part of that "more" here occurs within what poetry-savvy observers call the **Figurative** (representational; beyond the literal) level of the poem or lyric. This figurative or meaningful level thereby involves something more, in an extra dimension, deeper, which is usually addressed through poetic devices such as **simile** (references to similarities), **metaphor** (from European terms for the word "sign" or "indication", that evolved to indicate one thing and mean something totally different), **symbol** (sign, representation) and **allegory** (an extended metaphor or parable).[57, 93-4] The Moodies use these powerful poetic devices often, which we describe throughout this book.

4

As we make meaning we understand that there are two kinds: our *individual* takes on the meaning of the lyrics/poems *to each* of *us*, and what could be considered as a more general or universal meaning as understood by the most people.

When we **Interpret**, we look for the figurative or *meanings* in each song. We can do this *any time* that we listen to a Moodies' song. We decipher the meanings in more expanded detail than they are in the brief, concrete, yet sensuous and often more primitive but *underlying meaningful* language of the poem. When we begin to *think* about the words, we can begin to make the meaning that we discern, feel or get when we hear it in a song as it becomes clearer for us, especially when we read it.

EXAMPLE MAKING MEANING

As longtime listeners, we have made use of making meaning of the Moodies' lyrics available by going online and printing them out to have them available to us to read *as we listen to each song*. Sometimes we read them silently. When we interpret, we use our learned and inherent logic to decode and connect their poetic lyrics with our now extracted and expanded meaning. [93-4]

As an example, on the next page we make meaning of Mike's compelling poem. See if any of it rings true for you. While Pinder's words to this song are not as metaphorical or encoded as many other poems (e.g., see Robert Frost's "Stopping by Woods..." referenced above), we can still benefit

Table 1. Making Meaning of 'Have You Heard'
all three parts below by Mike Pinder 1969 from album OtToaD

Lyrics	Our Suggested Meaning
Now you know that you are real Show your friends that you and me Belong to the same world / Turned on to the same word Have you heard? Now you know that you are free Living all your life at ease / Each day has its always A look down life's hallways, doorways To lead you there	We are each only our Real Self, all of us. We can practice being real by showing our realness to ourself and one another every minute of every day. We are already and always free beings, pretending not to be free when we are afraid. We can stop being fearful and worrying so much. We can raise our consciousness and awareness one day at a time. We can do so through our raised awareness and by working through what we encounter in life every day.
The Voyage ~ Instrumental	Mike & the Moodies keep us in our mystical trance & take us deeper.
Part 2 Now you know how nice it feels /Scatter good seed in the fields Life's ours for the making / Eternity's waiting, waiting For you and me Now you know that you are real Show your friends that you and me Belong to the same world / Turned on to the same word / Have you heard?	When we do the above we feel good. We can spread that goodness by continuing to be real, aware, and work through our conflicts as they come up for us. It is our choice at every moment of every Eternal Now. We are already and always our real self, all of us. We can practice being real by showing our realness to one another, especially to safe people, every minute of every day. ...As you listen, you may be more aware of this wisdom.

from our own decoding of their message. Our interpretation moves from the concrete details of the poem (about being real, in this world, etc.) to more abstract statements about life ("We are already and always free beings to be real with ourself and others, especially safe others, and thereby enjoy our life" —see lyrics, Table 1 above).

Of course, not everyone will arrive at this exact understanding or interpretation, but something in this area is likely implied by the figurative language of Mike's poem. Our interpretation may not be yours. Or only some of ours may make sense to you. We can argue about specific details. Either way, of course, you are always free to make your own. Give us yours: moodiesbook.wordpress.com

About these three pieces music journalist and rock specialist Bruce Eder wrote: "This synthesis of psychedelia and classical music, including a section featuring Pinder on grand piano, may sound overblown and pretentious today, but in 1969 this was envelope-ripping, genre-busting music, scaling established boundaries into unknown territory, not only "outside the box" but outside of any musical box that had been conceived at that moment; perhaps it can be considered rock's flirtation with the territory covered by works such as Alexander Scriabin's *Mysterium*, and if it overreached, ...well, so did a lot of other people at the time, including Jimi Hendrix, the Doors, the Who, et al. To show the difference in the times, The Moodies even brought this extended suite successfully to their concert repertory, and audiences devoured it at the time. Amazingly, its album *On the Threshold of a Dream* was their *first chart-topping* LP in England, and remained on the charts for an astonishing 70 weeks." [19]

Interpretation looks for **meanings**, and in formal interpretation, meanings are often expressed in a more expanded way and clearer than they are in the particular language of the poem. Part of why the best poetry works, as the Moodies write and sing it so well, is that—as we read it or hear it sung to their mood-elevating music—our experience hearing it takes us into a trance which thereby *speaks* both *directly* to our conscious and *in*directly to our unconscious mind and body. If the words are real and positive, they are soul nourishing. Listening to them, *without even thinking* about them, we feel good. But when we read them as printouts of their original lyrics *and think* about them, we can thereby begin to make the meaning that comes up for us as we *feel, decipher* or "*translate*" their words, phrases and poetry.

'Have You Heard' may be Mike's most basic and telling song. We believe that it is one of his most mystical and powerful. His lyrics, vocal and instrumental delivery *with* his band mates' superb backing adds to the power of this amazing work. (He had first drafted it in December 1966 as part of a live stage act and later developed it, and the MBs finally published it in their 3rd core 7 album *OtToaD* more than two years later in April 1969). [61]

Making meaning of their lyrics can sometimes be simple. In a 1990 radio interview Justin said, "There is a double meaning within a lot of Moody Blues songs. There is that spiritual meaning, and then that 'I love you, come to bed Baby' meaning as well." [70] Here he acknowledges their songs' spirituality as well as their so often romantic flavor.

This whole process of interpreting and making meaning also correlates with where we may be in each of our own levels of consciousness, which we address below in Chapter 4.

The final standard or classical level of how poems impact us is by their **Sound**. Devices such as rhyme, rhythm, and alliteration help set and promote their mood and flow. But the Moodies don't just read their poems aloud. With their voices music and harmonies, they deliver their original lyrics—that *they have written themselves*—usually masterfully. If you are reading this book now and don't know what that word—masterfully—means here about their sound, you may consider listening to any of their core 7 albums now or soon, more than once. If you are a regular or past Moodies listener, you likely already know what we mean.

We also look more into the sound of their words and music in Chapters 12 through 15. In the next two chapters, as introductory examples, we look in some detail at the creative and often enlightening poetry in their first album, *Days of Future Passed.*

2 *DAYS OF FUTURE PASSED*: REFLECTIONS AND MEANINGS

Their first great work seemingly came out of nowhere to become a landmark in classic rock. It is remarkable that these five young men—who in their early twenties somehow came together (and synchronistically,[58] as we describe in Chapter 16) have composed such amazing and enduring poetry, music and message over several decades now. And yet more remarkable that their countless fans still follow them worldwide nearly 50 years later.

After two years as a struggling R&B band, in September 1967 executive producer Hugh Mendl asked them to record a rock adaptation of Dvořák's 9th Symphony as Decca's first stereo demonstration record. But the band wisely chose to focus on an album they'd been working on based on their original stage show about a typical person's typical day. (*Note*: Decca's recording engineer Derek Varnals said that even early in 1967 there was no intent to record a Dvořák album and that talk of such a project had not happened until the mid 1970s.) [71] Tony Clarke produced this and all of their later albums for the next 11 years, for which he was sometimes referred as the "6th Moodie."

How did that all start and happen? In a 2008 interview on their 1970 Isle of Wight concert DVD (see page 58), Justin said, "[During that time] We were singing about our lives. This was a time in our lives when we had nothing to do but music. We didn't have any money, we didn't have the big cars or the houses. All we did was make music. That's the difference. As you get older you get stuff, you get family, you get people around you, you get responsibilities, you've got to look after things. But then we had just music to do. And we were quite serious about that. We were *living* the music that we were playing every day. It was an expression of what was *in our hearts* and *in our souls*." [38]

They wrote *DoFP* in sequence. Justin said, "I had done 'Nights' already and Mike had done 'Dawn is a Feeling.' Then Ray said I'm going to do Twilight and the Morning. John said I'm going to do peak hour, the rush hour, and the evening time. That left the afternoon. So tomorrow was a Tuesday, I'm going into the field near my house and I'm going to write my song. And that's exactly what I did." [70]

When authors are inspired in varying ways, writing their poetic lyrics usually occurs as a stream of consciousness, from their unconscious mind. Most say that they may not know all the full meanings of their words at the time they write them.

Similar to conventional poetry, the meanings of song lyrics are subjective, in that the *listener* interprets according to their own experience. In the following pages we offer our interpretations of their poetic lyrics (Tables 2.1 and 3.1). Ours may not be yours, and, of course, you are always free to make your own understandings and meanings.

Table 2.1 Making Meaning of *Days of Future Passed*

Lyrics	Reflections and Meanings
The Day Begins Graeme Edge Cold hearted orb that rules the night Removes the colors from our sight / Red is gray and yellow, white But we decide which is right / And which is an illusion Pinprick holes in a colourless sky / Let insipid figures of light pass by / The mighty light / of ten thousand suns / Challenges infinity and is soon gone / Night time, to some a brief interlude To others the fear of solitude Brave Helios, wake up your steeds Bring the warmth the countryside needs	The first piece is a not a song but it is Graeme's poem that Mike Pinder reads, opening us with a psychospiritual statement *unique* in nearly all music. It contrasts day & night, light & dark, consciousness & unconsciousness. The size and wonder of the universe, reality and illusion, finite and infinite, meaning & meaningless. It closes by introducing the day with the sunrise (Brave Helios). Opens us to their signature mystical and spiritual message and delivery.
Dawn Is A Feeling Mike Pinder Dawn is a feeling A beautiful ceiling The smell of grass Just makes you pass / Into a dream You're here today No future fears This day will last	Mike here opens our typical person's typical day—though already mystical and spiritual—by a slow, sensual awakening. On interview he said that he was referring to the smell of actual fresh cut grass and not what others have interpreted, perhaps gleefully, although we

A thousand years If you want it to You look around you Things they astound you / So breathe in deep / You're not asleep Open your mind You're here today No future fears This day will last A thousand years If you want it to Do you understand That all over this land / There's a feeling / In minds far and near Things are becoming clear With a meaning Now that you're knowing / Pleasure starts flowing It's true life flies Faster than eyes Could ever see You're here today No future fears This day will last A thousand years If you want it to	may wonder because of the times (which was of course 1967). Then he introduces a major psychological and spiritual concept and reality: the present moment, the Now, the here-and-now, the Eternal Now—their clear introduction to *time*. Interspersed throughout their songs, the Moodies refer to time in many ways. His 4th stanza (S-4) You're here today... again reminds us of the Now. ** In S-5 he introduces the crucial reality of *consciousness* which we address in Chapter 4. He shows us that he is awake and that we can awaken too. He reflects on the awakening and opening of the late 1960s, including an expansion of our consciousness and making meaning in our lives. In S-6 he reminds us how good it feels to awaken, and in closing reminds us of the power of staying in the here-and-now.

Morning: Another Morning

Ray Thomas

Balloons flying
Children sighing
What a day to go
kite flying / Breeze
is cool
Away from school
Cowboys fighting
out a duel / Time
seems to stand
quite still / In a
child's world, it
always will

Fish is biting / So
exciting / Lunchtime
sounds so inviting
Angler Bill / He gets
a thrill / Sitting,
watching bobbing
quill / Time seems
to stand quite still
In a child's world, it
always will

Yesterday's dreams
Are tomorrow's
sighs / Watch
children playing
They seem so wise

Mary Green
Today is a queen
One thousand
dollies are a dream
In cotton frocks and
golden locks
Her palace is an
orange box

Repeat S-2

Here Ray jumps us into the morning of the day in the life of our ordinary person. Fanciful, seen through a child's eyes and experience; enthusiastic and fun.

Referring to *time* again "stand quite still," reminding us more on the here and now.

This is also their first reference to the power of our universal Child Within. In S-3 & 4, if you listen to the music here, they subtly introduce us to one of their captivating hallmark features: they move from a fast rhythm and beat to a slower one Yesterday's dreams... which immediately captures our attention. In S-3 Ray reflects more references to the wisdom of our Child Within and the Eternal Now.

In S-5 'Mary Green Today is a queen' Ray and other Moodies may know a meaning here. Otherwise, this is a fanciful departure from ordinary reality into his great whimsical poetry, a common characteristic of the Moodies' lyrics.

Final stanza: a repeat and reminder of the wisdom of our Child Within or Real Self as contrasted with the false self.

14

Lunch Break: **Peak Hour** John Lodge I see it all through my window, it seems / Never failing like millions of bees / All that is wrong, No time to be won, All they need to do What can be done Peak hour, Peak hour, Peak hour Minds are subject to what should be done / Problems solved, time cannot be won / One hour a day, One hour at night, Sees crowds of people All meant for flight. Peak hour x 3 It makes me want to run out and tell them, They've got time / Take a step back out, And look in, I found out, I've got time.... Repeat S-3 & s-4	A clear progressive rock song, here John dynamically explores our use of time, activity and productivity. Then more on time throughout this chronologically short but powerful song. 'One hour a day, One hour at night ...' and following brings us back into the here-and-now, called the *Eternal Now* by spirituality authors and scholars. John reminds us here that we can slow down, which now at his young age of 24 he has also discovered for himself. * → Time to turn over the vinyl LP, or the CD will continue

Notes to above table:
*In my (Barbara's) research into the after effects of the Near-Death Experience (NDE), people who have had these NDEs tend to talk the same way. Much of what he and the other Moodies refer to many times is in alignment with the after effects of the NDE and other spiritual awakenings, as we elaborate in Chapter 8.
**S = Stanza; S-1 = first stanza, S-2 = second, etc

In 2012, forty-five years later, John said, "...when we were making the album there was an energy in the studio I've never experienced before. Something special was happening, so much so that when we finished it, we put speakers on the side of the stage, and had an invited audience come along and listen to the very first playback. We sat there in the dark and it was pitch black, and we put the tape on and played the album for everyone. The album finished, and there was absolute silence. Everyone was mesmerized. When we heard that playback, we knew it was something special, but we never knew it was going to be commercial" [i.e., so commercially successful]. [13]

What was it like for you to read this chapter? What was it like for you to read our interpretations, and as you consider them with yours? Yours are just as valid as ours. What is important is that we all enjoy and appreciate their moving words and music. If you make other meanings than ours, consider sharing yours on: **MoodiesBook.Wordpress.com**

As we looked carefully at the meanings of the first poem and three songs above, we can now consider what the remaining songs said and meant to listeners and fans.

3 *Days of Future Passed*: **Reflections and Meanings** continued

Before addressing the rest of DoFP, let's pause and look at what these five critics have said about it.

Table 3.1 Critical Praise on *Days of Future Passed* [26]

Music Writer	Critic's Comments
Mark Moerman *Higher & Higher* mag. 1984	Nothing in their earlier work could have prepared us for this stunning leap into the furthest reaches of musical experimentation, nor for the remarkable impact it would have. [50]
Bruce Eder ...their most prolific journalist	... one of the defining documents of psychedelic [rock], and one of the most enduringly popular albums of its era. [17]
Robert Christgau 'Dean of American Rock Critics' [10]	... an essential album of 1967 "closer to high-art rock than psychedelia. But there is a sharp pop discretion ... and a trippy romanticism in the strings and Mike Pinder's Mellotron."
Will Hermes ...music critic & journalist	...an essential progressive rock record ...its use of the Mellotron made it a "signature" element of the genre. [31]
David Beard of *Goldmine*	...remains a *groundbreaking* album in combining rock music with classical. [4]

With their introductory poem and those three songs complete, we turn our vinyl LP over or continue on our CD, and listen as the Moodies resume with their next five songs and closing poem in this groundbreaking and landmark album. And we continue with how we can make meaning from our listening and reflecting on each of them for countless times over the decades.

Table 3.1 Making Meaning of *Days of Future Passed* *cont'd*

Lyrics	Our Suggested Meaning
The Afternoon: **Forever Afternoon (Tuesday)** Justin Hayward Tuesday afternoon I'm just beginning to see Now I'm on my way It doesn't matter to me Chasing the clouds away Something calls to me The trees are drawing me near I've got to find out why Those gentle voices I hear Explain it all with a sigh I'm looking at myself Reflections of my mind It's just the kind of day To leave myself behind So gently swaying Through the fairy-land of love If you'll just come with me And see the beauty of Tuesday afternoon Tuesday afternoon ... Repeats first 2 stanzas	Performed at most of their concerts. One of their most timeless, beautiful, and impactful of their poetry (similar to Knights in White Satin) seemingly also written in a stream of consciousness manner & flow. Could it reflect coming out of the fog of the effects of a weekend perhaps using psychedelics? After using one such as LSD on a Saturday or Sunday, not having slept for a day or two from the effect of the stimulating drug, Tuesday is a common time when our prior over-stimulated mind begins to become more clear. '...just beginning to see' Then, as a song-within-a song so beautifully woven in here, S-3 moves from a slow to a faster beat which captures our attention. Refers to unconscious material as many of their other songs' lyrics reflect.
Evening: **Time To Get Away** John Lodge Evening has come to pass	These are haunting and experiential lyrics and

18

The time of day doesn't last/ Evening has earned its place today, I'm tired of working away

Working, living it brings
Only way to have those things / Toiling has bought too many tears
Turn round all those past years

Evening time to get away x 3 / Till next day

Live all you people
You can see where you're at / It doesn't really hurt you / So that can't be bad

Evening time to get away
Repeat 4th stanza and Evening time to get away twice

melodies that are characteristic of their captivating musical art throughout this album and their next six classical, progressive rock masterworks.

John here writes less mystical and more ordinary words that are still true and experiential in our everyday lives, including the advantage of relaxing through our emotional pain.

Evening: **The Sunset**
Mike Pinder

When the sun goes down
And the clouds all frown
Night has begun for the sunset

See it with your eyes
Earth re-energized
By the sun's rays every day / Take a look out there / Planets everywhere

When the sun goes down
And the clouds all frown
Night has begun for the sunset

To start this groundbreaking album, Mike wrote its opening song—the dawn, and now addresses dusk, the night, evening poetry with a psychedelic or mind-expanding touch and flavor.

He continues his experiential and here mildly mystical path for us.

Shadows on the ground Never make a sound Fading away in the sunset Night has now become Day for everyone I can see it all From this great height I can feel the sun Slipping out of sight And the world still goes on / Through the night	Yet this piece remains as haunting as any in this ten piece (8 songs and 2 poems) new and special-in-all-of-progressive-rock "stage-show" group of psychological and spiritual compositions. It is a perfect segway into Ray's delightful 'Twilight Time.'
Evening: Twilight Time Ray Thomas Twilight Time, to dream awhile / In veils of deepening blue / As fantasy strides over colourful skies Of form disappearing from view / In twilight time, dream with me awhile A nightingale plays a dark mellow phrase / Of notes that are rich and so true An aerial display by the firefly brigade / Dancing to tunes no one knew In twilight time, dream with me awhile. Repeat Building castles in the air Whistling to the wind / As nature bows down her head See what tomorrow brings / Twilight time, dream with me awhile Bats take to wing, like puppets on string / Prancing through cool evening air In a sightless glide, no reason to hide / Away from the sun's blinding stare Repeat 4th Stanza (AKA S-4)	Deepening transition of day into night. More whimsical and fanciful, as Ray addressed in his lyrics so well and so often in this and his other outstanding songs. While Ray wrote no songs while in Band 1, compared to the their R&B days songs, this is more advanced and a big improvement in the words. And it is a giant improvement in its exceptional melody. Trance-like, this lovely song now takes us gently into the evening, preparing us for Justin's most played romantic love song.

Nights in White Satin The Night Justin Hayward Nights in white satin Never reaching the end Letters I've written Never meaning to send Beauty I'd always missed With these eyes before Just what the truth is I can't say anymore 'Cause I love you Yes I love you Oh how I love you Gazing at people Some hand in hand Just what I'm going through They can't understand Some try to tell me Thoughts they cannot defend Just what you want to be You will be in the end And I love you Yes, I love you Oh, how I love you Oh, how I love you Repeat 1st 2 stanzas and S-3 twice	From the imagination, heart and pen of a clearly creative 19-year old, this romantic ballad was an immediate hit. Said to be one of the greatest romantic love songs ever. Said it came from a recent break-up, a lost love that Justin had experienced. Classic free-form poetry. Stream of consciousness. This song taps into our collective and universal break-up-and-lost-love experiences that we have all had, plus our universal longing to give and receive love in general. From a deeper perspective our lost love can be that of our Real Self and our connection to God. "Just what you want to be You will be in the end" goes deeper and reflects our potentially increasing psycho-spiritual awareness, intention, and *self-responsibility* to grow and thrive.

Late Lament Graeme Edge	
Breathe deep the gathering gloom Watch lights fade from every room Bedsitter people look back and lament Another day's useless energy spent Impassioned lovers wrestle as one Lonely man cries for love and has none New mother picks up and suckles her son Senior citizens wish they were young Cold hearted orb that rules the night Removes the colours from our sight Red is grey and yellow, white But we decide which is right And which is an illusion. [this was the first stanza of The Day Begins above]	As Graeme began this unique first album of "a day in the life," he now ends with this appropriate poem, as read by Mike. Reflects on the day and some of our longings and wishes. He also ends with the mystical *first stanza* of his first poem here. Then more accompanying symphonic music ends this unique and powerful musical poetry that ended this premier album that launched their now nearly 50 year career.

Music journalist Bruce Eder said, "They came to this album with the strongest, most cohesive body of songs in their history, having spent the previous year working up a new stage act ...(and working the bugs out of it on-stage), the best of which ended up here." [17] The album's title *Days of Future Passed* was apparently first selected by Mike Pinder and of course approved or improved by the other four, as was said to have been the way they titled their remaining six core 7 albums. [33, 51]

Moerman wrote, "*Days of Future Passed*...was the starting point of the progressive rock movement to come to prominence a few years later with such groups as King Crimson and Yes. By this time the Beatles had released *Sgt. Pepper*, and the Beach Boys had done their classic *Pet Sounds*, both going well beyond the boundaries of the standard rock format. Both groups later returned to a much more basic sound ...*not the Moodies*. They not only went beyond these boundaries, they shattered them." [50]

Not only was *Days of Future Passed* a "catchy" title, but we believe that similar to their poetic lyrics, it has *multiple dimensions* embedded in its four otherwise simple words—had they not combined them as they did.

These dimensions include *time*, to which they often refer throughout their works (see also Chapter 15 below), the *here-and-now* (reflected in "day"—as in this typical day of a typical person) and their use of *consciousness*, which we begin to explore and address in the next chapter.

4 THE SPECTRUM OF CONSCIOUSNESS

In contrast to most bands and other music groups, in their lyrics and music the Moodies deliver a clear, consistent and high take on consciousness. Their own raised and timeless consciousness involve the source, focus, and delivery in their words and music.

Consciousness is our awareness of both our outer life and most importantly our inner life. It includes how awake we are to these aspects, our ability to experience and feel, having a sense of real selfhood, and it involves our own "executive" control system of our mind. Part of it includes anything that we are aware of at a given moment, making *conscious experience* at once the most familiar and most mysterious aspect of our lives. [36] (See the Appendix Glossary for more definitions.)

An interesting drawing on consciousness was by the 17th century English physician and metaphysician Robert Fludd as shown on the next page. While his terms were in Latin (and easily translatable), we include it to emphasize that consciousness is both *multidimensional* and *mysterious*. We have explored and studied consciousness for millennia. We have gradually learned enough to write about it and are slowly beginning to understand it better. Outside of our identifying ourself as being a body, consciousness is who we really are.

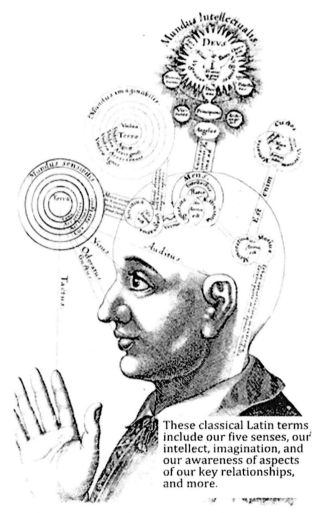

These classical Latin terms include our five senses, our intellect, imagination, and our awareness of aspects of our key relationships, and more.

Fig. 3.1 Drawing on consciousness
From Robert Fludd en.wikipedia.org/wiki/Consciousness

At the simplest view, our *body* houses our consciousness. But we know from near-death and other consciousness studies that it is already and always—and thus we can each exist—*well outside* of our earthly body.

Many spiritual sages, seekers and transpersonal (spiritual) psychologists have described and experienced three levels of consciousness: our lower self (ego), Real Self and Higher Self. They have also broken these into seven levels. In our and others' clinical experience we have shown how the stages of healing from illness parallel these. From our decades-long listening to the Moodies' profound words and music, in this book we include *selected examples* of their songs that we believe address each of these seven levels, whether they may have fully known of them or not (Table 4.1).

Table 4.1 Levels of Consciousness, Healing & MBs

Simple 3 Levels	Classic 7 Levels of Consciousness	Healing Stages	Moodies' Song Examples
Higher Self Love, Joy Peace Creativity Transcendence	7 Unity Consciousness.	3	The Land of Make-Believe
	6 Compassion		Candle of Life
	5 Understanding, Natural Knowing		Eyes of a Child
Real Self	4 Acceptance	2	Isn't Life Strange
Lower Self ego, false self, survival, emotional pain	3 Power/ego		You and Me
	2 Passion	1	And the Tide Rushes In
	1 Survival, neediness, unconscious	0	Gypsy ; Lost in a Lost World *

*Songs that open us to *all* of these levels – 'Out and In;' Stages 0 to 1 'The Actor' and Stages 1-2 'Say what you mean…. See numerous *Making Meaning* sections below, including in Appendix "Orchestra seating."

Mike and John's song 'Out and In' may be one of their most telling about their view of consciousness from several angles, as we summarize in the Table.

Table 4.2. Interpreting Their Song 'Out and In'

Lyrics	Reflections and Meanings
Out and In Mike Pinder Gazing past the planets Looking for total view I've been lying here for hours You gotta make the journey ... Out and in Wonders of a lifetime Right there before your eyes Searching with this life of ours / You gotta make the journey Out and in (repeat x 2) If you think it's a joke That's all right, Do what You want to do I've said my peace And I'll leave it all up to you Repeat S-2 Repeat S-3 Repeat S-1	We believe that this great song is about our journey *out* of our body and ordinary awareness and then *into* expanded consciousness. * To become fully conscious we have to wake up. We have to open *from* our ordinary awareness into letting go of our ego, letting go of needing to achieve superficially, get material goods, needing simply to survive, and let go *into* a journey into higher levels of awareness or consciousness. *A Course in Miracles* says: "The journey to God is merely the reawakening of the knowledge of where you are always and what you are forever. It is a journey without distance to a goal that has never changed." [88, 89] *Or, our* journey *out* of expanded consciousness and then back *into* it. * *

**depending on the two authors' or your the reader's understood meanings of these lyrics.

"Searching with this life of ours" describes how simply *living our life* over time is our way to attaining higher levels of consciousness. We use our pain, problems, conflicts, and any relationship difficulties as grist for the mill to heal and grow. We eventually make meaning out of working through our life's problems.

As Mike writes and sings so clearly, with his band mates,

> Wonders of a lifetime
> Right there before your eyes
> Searching with this life of ours
> You gotta make the journey
> Out and in

To fully appreciate the power of their work, play it on your sound system with your eyes closed and no distractions.

Consciousness scholars and practitioners Stuart Hameroff MD and physicist Sir Roger Penrose believe that consciousness has been a part of the Universe from its very beginning, an idea similar to the Buddhist and Hindu beliefs that consciousness is an integral component of the Universe. [28] Their theory is that quantum consciousness resides in the microtubules of our brain and that this quantum characteristic of the brain forms the soul.

In his delightful lyric poem, Ray addresses our early consciousness in 'Morning' from *DoFP*, "Time seems to stand quite still, In a child's world it always will," which we address next.

5 THE EYES OF A CHILD
"LISTEN, HEAR THE SOUND, THE CHILD AWAKES..."

From one of the Moodies' most praised core 7 albums, *To Our Children's Children's Children*, comes one of their most powerful psycho-spiritual works: 'Eyes of a Child,' written in early 1969 by John Lodge. This song opens us to two themes: the *child within* each of us and these five musicians' amazing *sounds*. We will address the child first.

The eyes of a child reflect those characteristics that most of us are born with and we can have at any age: innocence, spontaneity, non-judgment, trust, realness and love. But from our clinical work specializing in helping people who were repeatedly abused, traumatized or neglected, among them we have seen that these healthy qualities are too often and mostly lost. Our brief description below is a real but important departure from this book on the Moodies because we believe that their healing music and message are relevant for many of us who are trauma survivors. Bear with us a minute.

As a child, well over half of us were likely repeatedly mistreated, abused or neglected in varying degrees. [30, 87, 90, 91] To survive, our Real Self, True Self (Child Within) went into hiding (dissociated, separated) deep within the unconscious part of our psyche, as shown on the next page. To try to run our life, our false self (ego) took over. But it was not able to do the job. Over time, we may have felt more emotional pain, distressed, and at times even "crazy." Many of us have been mislabeled and mistreated with toxic psychiatric drugs that didn't work well. [91]

Figure 5.1 The Child Goes into Hiding

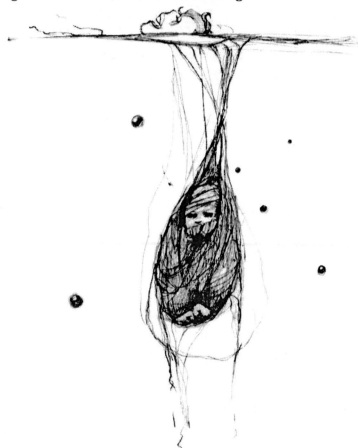

messages from impactful relationships "The Split"

Listening to the Moodies' music puts us trauma survivors into a healthy trance so that we can begin to hear their affirming and healing words. In a fair part of this book we address how this process happens, while, perhaps unknowingly, we have all enjoyed their music for so long without consciously exploring that process. In Table 5.1 below we interpret and make meaning of 'Eyes of a Child' by giving you our understanding of this powerful two-part song. To make reading it more impactful, as we do for interpreting and making meaning of *all* of their songs, we recommend that you play and listen to each of them as you read this here. Get out your copies of their great music and listen.

Table 5.1. Making Meaning of Eyes of a Child
both parts by John Lodge 1969

Lyrics	Our Suggested Meaning
Eyes Of A Child (part 1) Listen, hear the sound / The child awakes Wonder all around / The child awakes Now in his life He never must be lost / No thoughts must deceive him In life he must trust With the eyes of a child / You must come out and see That your world's spinning 'round And through life you will be A small part of a	Here the Moodies continue to show their view of our world through the eyes of a child. We said that the child in all of us has the powerful qualities of love, innocence, spontaneity, and trust; they are non-judgmental, real and creative. [87, 91] "Listen, hear the sound The child awakes" Through clearly hearing the sound of their words and music, the Child Within us (our Real Self) awakens to know that by being real with our self, *safe* others and God, that we will not be lost. "No thoughts must deceive him In life he must trust" And if we don't listen to our false

31

hope / Of a love that exists In the eyes of a child / You will see Earth falls far away New life awaits Time it has no day New life awaits Here is your dream And now how does it feel? No words will go with you And now what is real? **Repeat S-2**	self (i.e., ego –see the eerily smiling mask at the top of Figure 5.1) and trust the process, we will not be tricked or betrayed. "You must come out and see... And through life you will be A small part of a hope Of a love that exists ..." When we risk being child*like* and *real* with safe people we will find we are a small but real part of God's Love. "Earth falls far away... / ...New life awaits" When we let go of our attachment to our default-mode ego living and go into and with our real awakening experience, we will have a new healthy and loving life.
Floating Ray Thomas ...see lyrics online or on sleeve	Ray and the band sing and play an appropriate, childlike, whimsical and fun break here in the middle of this otherwise heavy two-part song.
Eyes Of A Child (part 2) I'm gonna sit and watch the web That you will build this day Will it be a thread of love you weave? It's yours to show the way Then everything will be As you will see in the light **Repeat S-2** **from part 1 twice**	With the beat speeded up, and with, in the background among their most glorious of harmonies, they encourage us to do what appears to be their main message: to say it and do it—live our life—with love.

We have now addressed above the first two of their messages and themes, the *child within* each of us.

The second involves these five musicians' amazing *sounds,* which we address in chapters *12* through 14 below.

But before that, in the next chapter we will go deeper and describe the Four Stages of healing as others and we understand them and we will begin offering examples of how selected of their best songs fit into each of these healing Stages.

Promo photo early on, probably taken in a studio [98]

6 THE STAGES OF HEALING AND THEIR MUSIC

In the late 1960s no one knew what we do now about the stages of healing, including the Moodies. Yet somehow in their words and music they addressed these levels seriously, especially Stage 3 recovery (the spiritual stage). In this chapter we begin to summarize the stages and introduce how their music connects to each of them.

Stage Zero When someone has a chronic illness, across a spectrum of addiction to a heart problem to diabetes or a disabling relationship problem, they are in what others and we have called Stage Zero. Here recovery and healing have not started. To review how the Moodies' songs can apply to each of these stages, look back at the bottom right of Table 4.1 in chapter 4, above.

Their two songs that we believe represent Stage Zero are 'Gypsy' and 'Lost in a Lost World.' In Table 6.1 on the next page we describe our take on 'Gypsy' and then in Table 6.2 on 'Lost... .' To make reading these more impactful, as we do for interpreting and making meaning of *all* of their songs, we recommend that you play and listen to each of them as you read here. As we said in chapter 1: Our interpretation may not be yours. Or only some of ours may make sense to you. We can argue about specific details. Either way, of course, you are free to make your own.

Table 6.1. Making Meaning of Gypsy by Justin Hayward

Lyrics	Our Suggested Meaning
Gypsy 1969 from TOCCC A gypsy of a strange and distant time Traveling in panic, all direction blind Aching for the warmth of a burning sun Freezing in the emptiness of where he'd come from Ahhhh, ahhhhh Left without a hope of coming home Speeding through a shadow of a million years Darkness is the only sound to reach his ears Frightening him with the visions of eternity Screaming for a future that can never be Ahhh, ahhhh Left without a hope of coming home Ahhhh, ahhhh **Repeat S-1** Left without a hope of coming home … x 2	This one of their most memorable and performed concert-set songs was originally planned by them to represent the U.S. astronauts' space travel to the moon in 1969. It starts us in the abyss of 'Lost…,' but by contrast these lyrics offer us no solution or way out. Justin here wrote such powerful and painful words as: strange, distant, panic, blind, burning, freezing, emptiness, left without a hope of coming home, shadow of a million years, darkness as the only sound, frightening, and screaming for a future that will never be. Strong words. Having assisted countless trauma survivors of repeated abuse and neglect from birth as they heal, we have heard this gestalt of pain from them over the years as they told their stories to us so often that we include this amazing song as representing Stage Zero. Listen to it again on your sound system when you have time.

We move next to 'Lost in a Lost World,' which continues to describe how it can feel when we are stuck in our default mode of ego attachment and pain. But this song *offers* us *a way out*, both of which we describe in Table 5.2 on the next page.

Table 6.2. Making Meaning of Lost in a Lost World
by Mike Pinder 1972 in *Seventh Sojourn*

Lyrics	Our Suggested Meaning
Lost In A Lost World I woke up today I was crying Lost in a lost world So many people are dying Lost in a lost world Some of them are living an illusion Bounded by the darkness of their minds In their eyes it's nation against nation against nation With racial pride Sad hearts they hide Thinking only of themselves They shun the light They think they're right Living in their empty shells Oh, can you see their world is crashing? Crashing down around their feet Angry people in the street Telling them they've had their fill Of politics that	Here Mike and the Moodies first address Stage Zero illness and pain. The pain reflects feeling lost, grieving (here crying), violence, and deterioration, most brought on by our attachment to our ego/false self. This remarkable survival oriented song first represents our lowest level of consciousness *as viewed from* a higher level: "Everywhere you go you see them searching Everywhere you turn you feel the pain Everyone is looking for the answer Well look again, come on my friend Love will find them in the end" - which now gives us an optimistic "glass half full" suggestion. So that even at our darkest, Mike and the band point us to our higher human qualities of searching for answers, especially for love, which most of their other songs also clearly address. They continue with a powerful solution almost never heard in rock music – the power of prayer: "Come on my friend We've got to bend

wound and kill

Grow, the seeds of evolution
Revolution never won
It's just another form of gun
To do again what they have done
With all our brothers' youngest sons

Everywhere you go you see them searching
Everywhere you turn you feel the pain
Everyone is looking for the answer
Well look again, come on my friend
Love will find them in the end
Come on my friend
We've got to bend
On our knees and say a prayer

Oh, can you see the world is pining
Pining for someone who really cares enough to share his love
With all of us, so we can be
An ever loving family

Have we forgotten we're all children?
Children from a family tree
That's longer than a centipede
Started long ago when you and I
Were only love

On our knees and say a prayer"

We may ask ourselves:
How many rock groups do we know who express this level of psychological, relationship and spiritual sophistication and maturity?

In the 6th stanza Mike and his band mates continue look from their higher consciousness at this lower Stage Zero level:
"Oh, can you see the world is pining
Pining for someone who
really cares enough to share his love
With all of us, so we can be
An ever loving family"

So even in this lowest consciousness and Stage Zero song, Mike and they still look for and at the solutions to being stuck in the pain of ego attachment.

Continuing to help us climb out of this abyss, they remind us by asking
"Have we forgotten we're all children?
Children from a family tree
That's longer than a centipede
Started long ago when you and I
Were only love"

This is strong songwriting made even stronger and more impactful by *hearing them sing it* within *their* soul-nourishing *music*.

Even though we have included this as a Stage Zero level as it relates to the stages of healing, Mike has inserted within four of its nine stanzas that *look upward* and

Repeat S-1	inward to the healing power of love—dare we say—of God's Love.
So many people, so many people, people Lost in a lost world So many people, so many people, people Lost in a lost world	To end, they bring us back downward into the abyss, reminding us how many of us may seem to be lost in that imagined & at times real feeling lost world.

If you have your own perspectives, interpretations or understandings of this song (or any other of their songs), consider posting them on our website blog that we have set up for you and others to share with us: **MoodiesBook.Wordpress.com**

In the next chapter we continue by describing Stage One healing and recovery and their songs that represent these opportunities so well.

7 STAGE ONE CONSCIOUSNESS, HEALING AND THEIR MUSIC

How many Moodies fans with various problems in living, including those with lasting illness, might you guess may get benefit from hearing their words and music? Chronic illness and pain are common. [87, 90, 91] Being in the heat of an unresolved conflict and trying to work through it is not fun. Repeated conflict is stressful, and repeated stress and distress cause illness. Still, we know that hearing good music can help us heal.

Stage One When someone has a Stage Zero chronic illness, whether a disabling addiction, a heart problem, diabetes or a serious relationship problem, when they begin to stabilize it so that it no longer disables them, they are entering Stage One recovery. Here, healing and recovery have begun and is starting to allow them to get substantial "breathing time." To review how the Moodies' songs can apply to each of these stages, look back again at the bottom right of Table 4.1 on page 26 above.

In our clinical and life experience we have seen how difficult and often dysfunctional relationships can negatively affect healing. Here below we show how our understanding of Ray Thomas' song 'And the Tide Rushes In' can apply in a difficult relationship problem conflict (Table 7.1).

Table 7.1. Making Meaning of And the Tide Rushes In
by Ray Thomas from their 1970 album *A Question of Balance*

Lyrics	Our Suggested Meaning
And The Tide Rushes In I've been searching for my dream A hundred times today I build them up, you knock them down Like they were made of clay Then the tide rushes in And washes my castles away Then I'm really not so sure When side of the bed I should lay I should lay... You keep looking for someone To tell your troubles to I'll sit down and lend an ear Yet I hear nothing new **Repeat S-2** Blackbird sitting in a tree Observing what's below Acorns falling to the ground He'll stay and watch them grow	Reading these lyrics, do they describe to you a couple in a conflict? Arguing painfully? If so, what is happening? Ray may be imagining having some conflicts with someone, most likely with whom he is in a close or an intimate relationship. Bruce Eder said it was likely Ray's first wife. [Eder] His partner does not appear to understand him, and she even rejects his ideas or expressions. It sounds like he experiences that she is not understanding him and may not be hearing him either. Their conflict sounds here like it is probably still unresolved for now: Then the tide rushes in And washes my castles away Then I'm really not so sure When side of the bed I should lay I should lay... Couples in this kind of repeated and painful conflict usually have not worked through their Stage Two issues (trauma effects), which we address later. They often remain attached to their ego during their conflicts. [90]

Most readers may know that the Moodies' songs address higher levels of consciousness. This next one continues to look at relationship difficulties, but from a more optimistic and higher perspective.

Table 7.2. Making Meaning of You and Me
by Justin Hayward and Graeme Edge from *Seventh Sojourn* 1972

Lyrics	Our Suggested Meaning
You And Me There's a leafless tree in Asia Under the sun there's a homeless man There's a forest fire in the valley Where the story all began What will be our last thought? Do you think it's coming soon? Will it be a comfort Or the pain of a burning wound? All we are trying to say Is we are all we've got You and me just cannot fail If we never, never stop You're an ocean full of faces And you know that we believe We're just a wave that drifts around you Singing all our	Justin (26 YO) and Graeme (31) start out poetically describing a primal nature scene where a homeless man represents each of us as once again almost 'lost in a lost world.' Our 'last thought' that they raise may turn out to be when, from painful relationships, we awaken to our need for healthy relationships. Back into our previous song's couple-in-conflict idea, they say, reminiscent of marriage vows, that if we stay committed to our relationship and stay together, we will succeed. What could these words mean? We look around in wonder At the work that has been done By the visions of our father Touched by his loving son To us they suggest a strong spiritual reference. Could the Father represent God? And the Son be the Christ? Or Christ consciousness that resides

hopes and dreams	in each of us—*as us*?
We look around in wonder At the work that has been done By the visions of our father Touched by his loving son Repeat S-3, 2 ½ times	As in 'Lost in a Lost World,' these words also point us upward—and inward within our soul—to the healing power of God's Love. Repeating stanza 3, 2.5 times, reminds us of the power of real commitment.

Most of their songs are about relationships, and especially love relationships—a subject rarely well written and delivered in rock music. While they occasionally and appropriately address emotional pain, in their words and message they tend to accentuate the positive. That with their healthy psycho-spiritual focus and loving and fun delivery, helps explain how they still have countless listeners and fans for nearly 50 years.

In others' and our long experience, most relationship problems are due to one and usually a combination of the following: 1) Having experienced repeated abuse or neglect as a child or older, 2) Growing up seeing unhealthy relationship skills or behaviors modeled to us by adults, 3) Attachment to our ego/false self (a temporary survival defense we learn in a troubled or lost world),   4) An active addiction—and now increasingly common since the Prozac era began in 1987— 5) The hidden but real and common toxic effects of psychiatric drugs. [90, 91]

An accessible venue through which to begin to address and heal around being in difficult relationships is the free-of-financial-cost Twelve Step fellowship of *Co-Dependents Anonymous* (see CoDA.org online).

We say more about relationship issues and how the Moodies address them in most of the chapters below.

Promo probably in Cobham, Surrey near the Threshold Studios [98]

8 THEIR MUSIC, SPIRITUALITY AND THE AFTER-EFFECTS OF THE NEAR-DEATH EXPERIENCE [1]

INTRODUCTION

In the two paragraphs below we want to give you some personal background information before we describe yet another key dimension of our understanding of their music and message.

By the time I (Barbara) was an adult, and until age 32 when I had a profound Near-Death Experience (NDE), I considered myself to be an atheist. Then, here's what happened. While suspended in a circle -frame bed after 5 hours of spinal surgery, my mind was forever changed by two experiences that I had near death. In that NDE I experienced being embraced by my grandmother who had died 14 years earlier and then embraced and merged with an Energy that I can now comfortably call "God."

Fast forward ten years and many synchronicities later when I became a researcher at the University of Connecticut School of Medicine with the two top NDE researchers in this field: Bruce Greyson MD and Kenneth Ring PhD. At that point we were mainly looking at the aftereffects of people who had touched death and returned to tell about it.

---

[1] Near-death Experiences or NDEs are also referred to as STEs (Spiritually Transformative Experiences). Coming close to death is one of several ways to experience an STE, as we show 2 pages below.

44

"By their fruits you will know them" became obvious as we tallied questionnaires and interviewed people who had had near-death experiences, as well as their close others. We also interviewed other people who came close to death and *didn't* have a near-death experience. We found that if they had an NDE, their fruits or aftereffects (as mine) clustered around *self-actualization*, *altruism* and *natural spirituality*, a natural connection to "something greater than ourselves." One other profound effect was an alteration in our perception of time, which we address in Chapter 15 on page 90. Whether we obtained their experiences on paper from research questionnaires or in face-to-face interviews, we and other investigators found that these aftereffects were almost always present and apparent.

THE MOODIES' RELATIONSHIP WITH STES
(Spiritually Transformative Experiences)

Our research at the university was during the 1980s. In the 90s I taught about these aftereffects at Rutgers University's Institute for Alcohol and Drug Studies. At both the University of Connecticut and Rutgers, when I brought up romantic or spiritual music that reflected these aftereffects, the Moody Blues were sometimes mentioned, and often enough in the same breath as Beethoven's Ninth Symphony and the new age music of Iasos (Angels of Comfort). Iasos and much of Beethoven had the mood and the Moodies had the *ideas* in their *words* enfolded in their music.

We mentioned their music and lyrics recently on a near-death experiencer internet discussion blog. Many wrote how they have followed the Moodies over the years because of the similarities among their lyrics and their own post-NDE values and life changes (*self-actualization*, *altruism* and *natural spirituality*) and also for those who have had spiritual experiences brought on other ways. **Triggers** for STEs (Spiritually Transformative Experiences) include: 1) experiencing the death of a loved one, 2) childbirth, 3) deep prayer, 4) overwhelming loss, 5) detoxifying from alcohol and other drugs, 6) working a Twelve Step fellowship program, 7) regular meditation, 8) NDEs 9) some psychedelic drug experiences and 10) dare we say, listening to and letting go into the Moodies' words and music. These experiences each have included the same aftereffects we named above. [86]

Although Ray told us that he did not write it for this reason, [77] our first of many examples referring to the aftereffects is in his song 'Legend of a Mind:' "Timothy Leary's dead. / No, no, no / He's outside, looking in." While Ray said that he meant no such connection to NDEs, his imagery paints a picture that many of us describe at the beginning of our near-death experiences. We are out of our bodies looking at our physical body, which appears to be "dead," or at least well on the way to death. We could be looking at our loved ones who are reacting to our death, or at the medical staff who were working quickly to try to revive us. And what we wanted to tell them (but they couldn't hear us) is "Oh No! We are out here, looking in."

A few of the Moody Blues spent some time with Timothy Leary who was a proponent of using psychedelic drugs selectively, especially LSD. [37] Ray said, "I was very fond of Tim Leary, I have nothing bad to say about him and we never took LSD together." [77] Even though using psychedelics was legal at that time, he was pushed out of Harvard for unclear reasons where he was a lecturer in psychology. He spent many years, both at Harvard and then in the public domain "turning people on" to the spiritual experience of psychedelics, at times by being "a sitter." A sitter is someone who understands the terrain or the journey and helps another glean the best results from the experience, often referred to as coordinating set and setting, being in a safe place with a guide who helps the traveler to go out and then safely come back in (see also our interpretation of their song 'Out and In' above).

Leary said that psychedelics in proper doses and in a stable setting guided by a psychologist, could improve one's life. His research looked at using it to treat alcoholism and possibly to reform criminals. Many of his research subjects spoke of having profound mystical and spiritual experiences that they said improved their lives. [37]

Our next example showing that the Moodies had a profound spiritual life changing experience (STE) is in another song, 'Out and In.' Our research shows repeatedly that we were really out there and came back in. [86] Some if not many of us learned quickly to meditate as a way to go "out there" to a higher level of consciousness and then come back "In." Yoga, Tai Chi and some other martial arts gave us this needed "Out and In" experience, as well as for any of us who may have used psychedelics (more on that below).

But more than needing to go out and in, many of us turned to altruistic endeavors as a way to fill this need which we can call "engaging in something greater than ourselves." When we voluntarily "pay it forward" to someone who needs it, there is a metaphoric and real sense of going 'Out and In.'

In 'English Sunset' we hear their awareness of consciousness: "I feel the rhythm of the Earth in my Soul tonight." This is a perfect example of what near-death experiencers often talk about when we get together. Our senses are heightened, including some that are being explored and documented by a new science, parapsychology. Parapsychologists study a number of paranormal phenomena, such as near-death experiences telepathy, precognition, clairvoyance, and reincarnation.[56] In this same stanza Justin sings that he has decided to live with humility, a goal that near-death experiencers travel toward and that many eventually embrace. This trait of *humility* is so important that in 2005 we wrote about it in our book *The Power of Humility: Choosing Peace over Conflict in Relationships.*

'Haunted' is another song that at first we thought was about a woman who had left and broken someone's heart. But the more we listened, the more we considered it, as many of us may also, that instead of being solely about a woman, it was also about God's love that we felt in our NDEs and STEs and can't find easily here in this reality. Some of the key words that express the aftereffects of longing for that relationship with a Higher Power or God in an NDE or STE are:

> I really miss you when the nights are long
> And only silence is heard in this world of song
> But life goes on
> And forever more I'll be haunted by your love
> I see you walking through the gates of home
> And then I wake up to find I'm still all alone
> I should have known
> But forever more
> I'll be haunted by your love

And of course, the one immediate and most important value of the Moody Blues and those who have had a *spiritually transformative experience* is **Love.** This word is central among their lyrics and to nearly all who have an STE. All of my books, all of our research into the NDE, and most recently former Harvard neurosurgeon Eben Alexander's book *Proof of Heaven,* confirms that we are here to understand Unconditional Love and even more importantly to live it. Hundreds of books and articles have been written about the NDE and STEs and all of the authors would agree that if we had to boil it down to one word it would be Love.

Mike Pinder sums up the Moodies take on love in 'My Song.' He writes, "Love can change our destiny / Love can change the world / Love can change your life / Do what makes you happy / Do what you know is right! / And love with all your might." (see More Making Meaning in the Appendix, p 152).

In their several songs about children, the Moodies words have taught us and countless others once again to see through the eyes of a child. One of our teachers said that to enter the kingdom of Heaven, we must become as a little child (as in their 'Eyes of a Child'). Their lyrics remind us why it is such a joy to be caregivers for our grandchildren. Lily coming to us every day is a gift and gateway into the bliss that the Moodies remind us of.

Sometimes watching a concert in the evening when Lily comes to visit us while her parents have a "date night" is a treat. She sits between us entranced by a Moodies concert on a DVD. When she was three she knew most of them by name and knew several songs she wanted to see and hear. She sometimes fell asleep as they performed and we carried her to bed with their songs of love in the background.

From others' and our consciousness research, from our own personal experiences and from the experiences we have shared with each other and our grandchildren, their lyrics express clearly and blissfully what life here on this planet is really all about when we reach for the spiritual.

CHANGING THE WORLD

I remember when I first joined the non-profit board for the *International Association for Near-Death Studies*, we thought we were going to change the world with our study of the NDE's aftereffects. People who have died and come back knew things about the purpose of life that most don't know. We don't know if we had any influence through our books and our occasional TV and radio appearances.

But we do know that listening to the Moodies has helped us and countless others to change ourselves and our relationships by their singing and living these aftereffects. They and each of one of us do so by telling the world about higher consciousness and how to get there. That way is by healing ourselves enough that we can love each other in a healthy way, love something greater than ourselves and also love ourselves through healthy self-caring. These timeless troubadours are singing what those of us who have had a direct experience of a "Higher Power" are trying to express and embrace.

MIND EXPANSION

The term *psychedelic* is derived from the Greek and means mind expanding or soul-manifesting. Graeme said "Everyone...was interested in mind-expanding...then [during the late 1960s and early 70s]." [38] Justin added "We were going through a lot of religious and psychedelic experiences together. I think we were seeking and searching for some kind of enlightenment in our lives. ...I think that's a worthy occupation for a young man. Back then I used LSD 10 or 12 times. I'm glad I did." [36, 38, 41] While many other bands also used psychedelics similarly, most of them did not appear to reach the same higher levels of consciousness in their lyrics and music as the Moodies.

As a near-death experiencer myself (BW), and a researcher in this field for over 30 years, I find it interesting and puzzling that of all the bands that started in the 60s, only The Moody Blues appeared to have found that high a level of consciousness from their psychedelic drug experiences. Most rock bands of that era openly talked about taking psychedelics but it is only in the Moodies music that we find such an evolved level of understanding of what our life here is really all about. The other bands may have tried, but there is nearly always that "edge" of harshness, even toying with the dark side. The Moodies may express the occasional heartbreaks of life but they don't flirt with darkness, don't smash their guitars or wear weird make up. Over and over they prove themselves as being a band that gives us a higher order of words, music and message. Viewing several of their videotaped and print interviews we have seen that they aren't just singing about their and our altruistic and personal changes, but they are also living them, which appears to separate them from most other bands.

While doing research at the University of

Connecticut Medical School, we looked at whether any NDErs had experienced repeated childhood trauma. At my suggestion, Ken Ring included several questions on what he called "Unpredictable violence in Childhood" among his surveys. He found that over half of NDErs reported unpredictable violence, which appears to be significantly higher than those who came close to death without having an NDE and those who never came close to death.

In the next several chapters we continue this theme of childhood (and other) repeated trauma to show that the Moody Blues are singing about the levels of healing that those of us who experienced repeated trauma have gone through. It seems that, for us as NDErs (and STErs) and for other spiritual seekers, the Moodies are aware of the humility needed to move toward self-actualization. And in their music they express that wisdom, both subtly in many dimensions and clearly in other ways that we describe throughout this book.

9 LEVELS OF LISTENING

Before we look at and make meaning on more of their songs at the next higher levels of consciousness and healing, let's step back and explore different ways of appreciating their music and message.

OUR STORY OF HEARING AND LISTENING

Most of us know that there is a difference between hearing and listening. Hearing their music in the background without focusing on it to any degree is how Barbara and I began it. Starting at the *bottom* of Table 9.1 two pages below we can see how perhaps *most* of us began hearing their music. Can you remember when you first heard them? I (CW) had lived in London for a year in 1971-2 while doing a postgraduate fellowship in medicine, but didn't know of their music—*or* that I might have been able to see them in concert there.

On returning to the States, I first heard them from a vinyl LP playing in a friend's house in 1973 and remember asking them who these guys were. That fast, I was already starting to enjoy *hearing* them, but was not yet interested enough to listen consciously to their words or message. But there was clearly something about their sound that engaged me. I heard them off and on over the next few years, and in 1977 I bought an LP album of *DoFP* (there were no CDs until 1982) and eventually a few more, including *Octave*. But I still did not listen carefully.

I always knew early on that I was stirred by them. I saw one of their first concerts live in 1977 or '78 when they got back together, and remember that they didn't seem to miss a beat. I bought more of their music over time. I was disappointed that, after their core 7, I enjoyed fewer of their new songs. It was only in the late 1990s when I saw and heard some of their concerts on DVD that I started to really listen to the words and the often profound ideas embedded in their lyrics.

I had met Barbara in 1990. She slowly started hearing the tapes and CD Moodies' "favorites" I had compiled from my collection. Later, as we watched their DVD concerts together, we started paying more attention to their lyrics and eventually to their message. I searched the web for their lyrics (long in the public domain) [25] and printed them for us to read both alone and as we were listening to each song. In late 2008, while we watched their DVD concerts more, we realized that their message and story were too important and compelling for us as long-published authors not to address.

There are almost countless similar testimonials and stories from fans and listeners of all experiences. Many of these are available online and some were published in print, as in *Higher & Higher* magazine from 1983 through 1992, and elsewhere. [50, 51, 55] But most of these are still unpublished and remain in *your* own life as valid experiences and stories. What is your story of discovering, listening and enjoying these timeless troubadours?

Table 9.1 Levels of Hearing and Listening

Level	Description and Comments	Ambiance Experienced
7 Transcending and integrating its message in living a joyful, peaceful and loving life	We apply their message of peace, joy and love to our everyday life.	Our personal life becomes more loving and joyful. Their music can become a part of the soundtrack of our life
6 Applying its message to our life	We use their message for the positive aspects of our life	We see and experience their metaphors in our everyday life
5 Pursuing continuing to enjoy and appreciate their words and music	We listen more often and may go still deeper into their words, melodies, and their message and meaning	Expansion to the point where the words & melody are playing in our "mind's ear"
4 Listening carefully for the message	We begin hearing parts of their *lyrics* in our "mind's ear." We begin to hear one or more parts of their *message*	Opens our hearts and mind as we begin to "see" on a deeper level
3 Listening carefully to some of the words	We begin hearing parts of the *melodies* and rhythms in our "mind's ear." After a while, we start to pay attention to some of the words.	Concepts are opening us to new possibilities and insights
2 Enjoying the music	We like it or take pleasure hearing it and may want to hear it more	Begins to open us to new feelings and stirrings
1 Hearing it in the background	This is how most of us begin hearing their music Can help create an ...	... enjoyable or peaceful environment

So here we are: documenting in this book what we have learned about them and what meanings we have made about their great words and music. Even though we have now finished writing this book, their works are so rich to us that we continue to listen for our simple enjoyment and still at times for the meanings we may make of their songs.

EXPERIENCING THEIR CONCERTS IN PERSON AND ON DVD

Have you attended a concert or viewed one or more on DVD that had excellent quality sound? If you did or can, we can tell you that we have experienced something remarkable, coming from a non physical dimension that is higher and yet almost palpable that we have to experience directly to know. Personally, we felt as though God's Love and Light of Consciousness opened us to a sensitivity that has remained with us to this day.

We can write and read about it. But to truly understand and know it, we have had to experience it. We believe they are bringing into this reality a gift from a Higher Reality, call it God's Grace, or timeless moments where we feel something bigger than them coming through their words and music.

We list and summarize the DVD documentaries, concerts and a radio interview that we have seen and listened to in Table 9.2 on the next two pages.

Table 9.2. Concerts and Documentaries on DVD & CD

Concert on DVD	Description and Comments
The Lost Performance: Live in Paris 1970	Earliest concert documented on a DVD. Has the expected visual and auditory graininess. Still worth a look, with good low prices on Amazon and elsewhere.
Threshold of a Dream: Live at the Isle of Wight Festival August 1970 (released 2009)	Far better quality, 9 songs with 1908-9 commentary by GE, JL, JH, MP. Best *Legend of a Mind* we have ever seen or heard. A must view. Worth owning.
Countless YouTube songs from Wembley to Red Rocks concerts and beyond	Vary in quality but when you have free time they are worth sampling. Include many interviews and Justin's British *This is Your Life.*
The MBs Story Feb 1990 radio, music and interviews, on CD	Among others, 3 hours of a Feb 1990 radio show in Philadelphia by Ed Sciaky, with annoying commercials.
Live at Montreux France 1987	Fair visual quality, but low sound quality. Still worth a look if serious fan.
Live at Red Rocks '92 with Colorado Symphony	19 songs in good quality video and sound (released in 2002)
Live from the Royal Albert Hall, London 2000	14 songs in high quality video & sound (released in 2002)
Lovely to See You live Greek Theater in L A 2005	20 songs in high quality video & sound (released in 2008)
Classic Artists text by Bruce Eder **Inside the Music**	Two good DVD documentaries with MBs, sound engineer Derek Varnals, producer Tony Clarke, and various commentators and critics such as journalist Keith Altham, Tony Brown, former MB keyboardist Bias Boshell, etc, blended with some songs (released in 2009). May be worth owning for serious fans.

Moody Blues Videobiography a take-off from above 51 min. 2007	Apparently an unauthorized video/biography; excludes EGBDF. Advertizes comes with a 48-page booklet with track-by-track analysis of every Moody Blues recording, but we have not found that.
Moody Blues Collected won't play on all DVD players	16 classic video clips 1967-88; Retitled and reissued version of 'Nights in White Satin' many unique to this DVD
Future DVDs ?	Keep a lookout & let us all know

Over the years we have gotten so used to many of their lyrics and what they mean to us, that sometimes, when something out of the ordinary is happening for us, we hear their words playing in our inner life or our "inner ear." Has anything like that ever happened to you? We have found that if we pay attention, there is often an underlying message about what is or may be going on for us in our outer life or perhaps more often inner life. And that message is often more spiritual in nature than not, including when we identify any synchronicities (see Chapter 16 and the Appendix) we may notice.

Consider sharing any of your experience listening or reading our book on our website

MoodiesBook.Wordpress.com

or as part of a brief review of this book on Amazon.com or any Moodies page

10 HEALING RELATIONSHIPS: STAGE 2 RECOVERY IN THEIR MUSIC

In this chapter we will address the first two of our three most important relationships: those with 1) others and 2) our relationship with our self. (The third important relationship is with God, or if you prefer God/Goddess/All-That-Is, or as Twelve Step fellowship members often say, 'the God of our understanding.' We will focus on that in Chapter 18 on Stage 3 consciousness, healing and spirituality).

When the Moodies wrote their core 7 albums' lyrics, from 1966 to '72, they would not likely have known about a Stage 2 healing because that observation had not been made until the late 1980s. [30, 87. 90] But some people knew about the detrimental effects of repeated trauma on relationships that are common worldwide, and an enterprising and existentially insightful poet of that time could have written well in varying degrees on this issue. And that is exactly what the Moodies appeared to us to have done—and to a fairly high degree at that, as we will show below. Their songs also addressed some *key issues* in relationships, which we also describe in this chapter and throughout this book.

But first, some more background. And remember that we can understand this all from the perspective of the Eyes of a Child, as we began to cover in Chapter 5 above. In Stage 2 healing and recovery we work through our trauma effects that developed from how others have treated us as children *and* over the rest of our lifetime. In Stage 2 we also address any of our relationship problems.

The typical motivation for beginning Stage One recovery is hurting too much—emotional pain, physical pain or debilitating disease, which we call Stage Zero illness—where healing and recovery has not yet started. But eventually, somewhere during, or more often *after* Stage One recovery, people may realize that they are still hurting. They realize that whatever they have done before hasn't worked as well as they had hoped—that the Stage One approach alone (conventional medicine, drugs, surgery, etc) didn't help them enough, or they may actually have gotten worse. So they might then be more open to exploring other alternatives. That situation is where they can begin a more substantial healing—*if* they are able to find ways to do that and especially if they find a helping professional clinician who *knows* Stage Two work.

Stage Two recovery involves naming, working through, and healing the effects of repeated childhood and later trauma, including working through related core issues. [90] A trauma survivor may have grown up in an unhealthy, troubled or dysfunctional family and/or world. Many may still be in a similar unhealthy environment, whether at home, in one or more relationships, or at work. Others and we have described how to recognize these situations and how best to heal from them. [30, 87. 90] We will here address them only through how the Moodies have done so well in some of their key songs about our all-too-human and common relationship difficulties.

We know that the history of music is replete with little stories about relationships. Throughout the history of lyrical music, from opera to pop to country music, these many and varied aspects of our relationships and their related problems seem to be repeated in song after song. We believe that the Moodies rank among the rare masters at portraying the reality of our drama *and* that they eventually show us the ideals of some of the healthiest relationships.

As perhaps many of you, we have listened long to their words and music and have seen how they show us these many and common relationship experiences. That common experience among us listeners and fans may help explain why for nearly five decades we have continued to enjoy their psychologically, spiritually and soul-nourishing musical message.

In the following tables we use selected of their songs to illustrate these timeless principles. We start with 'The Voice' from their 1981 album *Long Distance Voyager*. We see a lot of psychological and spiritual wisdom written by Justin when he was about 35 years old and married for 15 years with a 13 year-old daughter. This piece has a similar great melody as 'Nights...' and 'Tuesday Afternoon,' but it delivers a clearer and more detailed message about painful relationships, which is the focus of Stage Two consciousness and healing.

Table 10.1. Making Meaning of The Voice

by Justin Hayward from *Long Distance Voyager* 1981

Lyrics	Our Suggested Meaning [30, 87]
The Voice Won't you take me back to school? / I need to learn the golden rule Won't you lay it on the line? / I need to hear it just one more time Oh, won't you tell me again / Oh, can you feel it? / Oh, won't you tell me again tonight Each and every heart it seems / Is bounded by a world of dreams / Each and every rising sun / Is greeted by a lonely one Repeat S-2 'Cause out on the ocean of life my love / There's so many storms we must rise above / Can you hear the spirit calling? / As it's carried across the waves #6 You're already falling / It's calling you back to face the music / And the song that is coming	In 2013 Justin said about it, "I used to feel a lot of guilt about our position in the world and that we were really privileged and that went into that song." [69] But we see much more here. One of Justin's best lyrics starts out with a well-known basic principle in relationships: 'Do unto others…' which we see as setting the stage for us getting honest with ourself and others to introduce his message. This is the clear and basic start of healing any relationship conflict or pain. Here he reminds himself *and* us by this stanza and then by repeating it 5 more times throughout the song. In our life journey we have wishes and feelings, often including loneliness every day as we awaken: Each and every rising sun / Is greeted by a lonely one. Then he repeats the above reminder. But what are we lonely for? What is missing? In our life we encounter so many difficulties and there is a spirit calling us about how to handle our pain. [What is the nature of that spirit? Is it a Higher Power? God?] That spirit is everywhere - carried across the waves. We awaken to *our* unconscious mind

through / You're already falling / The one that it's calling is you	or spirit 's assistance by saying that we are 1) the experiencer of our drama, here called 'the music,' *and* we are 2) the one who calls us to heal, *and* that
Make a promise, take a vow / And trust your feelings, it's easy now Understand the voice within / And feel the change already beginning Repeat S-2 twice	3) we are our own healer if we commit to it by Making a promise, take a vow / And trust our feelings by going within to hear our Real Self/Child Within/Eyes of a Child expressing our authentic inner life [beliefs, thoughts, feelings, wants, healthy needs, memories, unconscious material, unfinished business] —all helped by our connection to God /Spirit.
And how many words have I got to say? / And how many times will it be this way? / With your arms around the future And your back up against the past	So by doing the above, how many times will we have to tune in to our real inner life? All we have is our experience in the Now (i.e., With your arms around the future And your back up against the past as clearly defining the present moment).
Repeat S-6 Re[peat S-3, then S-2 twice	
Oh, won't you tell me again tonight. Tonight	So each time we find ourself in another conflict or make another mistake, we can just remind ourself that we can recycle by reinstituting these above skills. ...All, powerful healing words.

What was it like for you to read our suggested meanings on this song? Did you have a different understanding of it? Another take on it? We see it as one of Justin and the Moodies' most evolved songs for all the reasons we say in the table.

The next song addresses a common factor in relationship problems and a core issue. [90] Being real with one another is a basic dynamic among healthy relationships, here for us as 'No More Lies.'

Table 10.2. Making Meaning of No More Lies

by Justin Hayward 1988 from *Sur La Mer*

Lyrics	Our Suggested Meaning
No More Lies I need you like you need me / Truly and completely / Never be apart / I think that you should tell me / Come right out and tell me / Just what's in your heart And if you think that it's alright / Let's make a deal and work it out We'll walk into the sunset you and I With no more alibis / When we tell each other No more lies Well truth is my addiction / Stranger still than fiction / Wider than the sky And songs that have such feeling / Words that have such meaning / Dreams that never die ...3 more Stanzas here And if you think that now feels right / Let's close the door and dim the light / We'll greet the dawn together side by side / Just look into my eyes / Cause you know I'll tell you / No more lies	Of course these words describe the relationships that most of us wanted. An ideal in any throughout our life. But how many times have we experienced one? Here we hear Justin saying he wants a relationship wherein he and the other are always real with one another. (Lying spans a wide spectrum from fibs to 'white lies' to clear untruths.) [42] We have written widely about the Real Self/Child Within as opposed to the false self/ego (see Table 10.3). So how can I tell if the other is telling me the truth? Our experience is that there is no 100% sure way to tell without experimenting, using trial and error or a share-check-share approach. To risk being real with people takes *courage, motivation, awareness* and the *discernment* to seek out and find *safe* others. To do that is not always easy. It takes practice and trial and error. We summarize some basic characteristics of our Real Self as compared with our false self/ego in Table 10.3. Justin poetically and romantically tells us in this Stage 2 consciousness and healing song what he wants in a healthy relationship.

Take a minute or two in the table below and study these characteristics that differentiate our real from our false self. We see the Moodies' words and music as representing our Real Self, for which we give examples in this and the next chapter.

Table 10.3. Some Characteristics of our Real Self and false self/ego [87, 88, 90]

Real Self	false self
Authentic Self, True Self	Unauthentic self, mask, persona, ego
Genuine	Un-genuine, "as-if" personality
MB's works *represent* it	**MB**s show us *how to transcend*
Spontaneous	Plans, plods or impulsive
Expansive, loving	Contracting, fearful
Giving, communicating	Withholding
Accepting of self and others	Envious, critical, idealizes, perfectionistic
Compassionate	Other-oriented, conforming, co-dependent
Feels feelings, including appropriate spontaneous, current anger	Denies or hides feelings, including long-held anger (resentment)
Ability to be child-like	may be childish
Needs to play and have fun	Avoids play and fun
Vulnerable	Pretends always to be strong
Powerful in true sense	Gives power away
Trusting	Distrusting
Private self	Public self

11 HEALING RELATIONSHIPS: STAGE 2 CONSCIOUSNESS...CONTINUED

This is such a crucial issue in attaining healthy relationships and a frequent enough topic among the Moodies' songs that we continue giving more examples here. We start with a common request.

Table 11.1. Making Meaning of Say What You Mean
by Justin Hayward 1991 from *Keys of the Kingdom*

Lyrics	Our Suggested Meaning
Say What You Mean 1 Say what you mean Mean what you say *... Repeat above* Think about the words That you're using Speak for yourself Say what's on your mind / Think about the life / That you're choosing / Whenever you need somebody Whenever you're looking / For somebody who knows When trouble won't leave you alone. 2 Repeat 1st 2 lines Look into the world of tomorrow / Say what you want / Want what is true / Check out of the room / Full of sorrow / I'm ready to take you with me	This is a two-part song about 8 minutes long. It has a captivating beat with synthesized strings in the background reminiscent of Electric Light Orchestra. In part 2 in the background it has an unknown voice reciting a poem that is difficult to hear clearly but which subliminally adds to its intrigue and romance. This phrase Say what you mean and Mean what you say applies to all kinds of relationships, not just intimate or committed ones. These can include our relationships with our friends, relatives, teachers, co-workers, bosses, neighbors and most others. It includes our important relationship with ourself too. [68] These lyrics may appear to be an extension or continuation of what Justin and the Moodies began in 1988 with their song 'No More Lies' in their 12th album *Sur La Mer* as we showed in the prior chapter. And these words

I'm ready to be the one
Who's there by your
side / When you've
just got
Nowhere to hide.

3 And oh, / The angels
will walk with you
Whenever you need
them / Yeah, the glory
that comes with love
Yeah, yeah, yeah
And oh, / The treasure
that waits for us
Whenever we need it
Now, I just can't hold it
back Yeah, yeah, yeah

4 The work and the
pain / The thunder and
the rain / The word of
the earth has been
spoken / The bird on
the wing / Free as the
wind / Knowing that
the spell / Has been
broken / Now you can
laugh with meaning
Now you can throw
away / The cloak of
disguise / As you turn
your face To the sky

5 The blue of the night
The secrets of the light
The touch of the hand
That can lead you / I
know you recognize
The shiver of surprise
Then you realize
That he's seen you Into
the strange unknown
of love Standing before
me /How your
nakedness shows /

here also describe the interpersonal
dynamics in relationships that most of
us wanted.

In this song we hear Justin again
saying he wants a relationship
wherein he and the other are always
real with one another.

Rather than just 'Don't lie to me,' he
expands that request to 'Say What
You Mean' —be clear and real with
me.

Justin poetically and romantically tells
us in this Stage 2 consciousness and
healing song what he wants in a
healthy relationship. *Part 2* of this
song repeats the same lyrics as Part 1
and then adds two more main
stanzas-

7 Let's walk into the forest
Only witnessed by the moon
And the breeze that once would chill us
Now excites
Say what you mean, mean what you say

8 And we'll touch the secret places
As the earth beneath us breathes
And the raw exquisite ecstasy
Rushes in
Say what you mean, mean what you say
Yeah, yeah, yea

These two stanzas add still more
intrigue and romance.

This is relationship wisdom disguised
as a snappy upbeat romance tune.
But it may hit some of us in our
creative unconscious mind enough to
remind us of this important phrase
Say what you mean and Mean what you say.

Now I just can't leave you alone 6 Ah oh, / I'm ready to take you now Whenever you want to go / Yeah, my heart is there for you Yeah, yeah, yeah And oh, / he glory that comes with love For always and ever, now / Now you can feel me love Yeah, yeah, yeah x2 Repeat 1st 2 lines Tell me about the love that you're feeling Repeat 1st 2 lines	A problem for many is that they are not healed sufficiently to be able to be so real as these words say. [68] Difficulty being real is a common core issue in relationships. There are some 14 *other* core issues: Needing to be in control, All-or-none thinking and behaving, Difficulty handling conflict, Fear of abandonment, Neglecting my own needs, High tolerance for inappropriate behavior, Grieving my ungrieved hurts, losses and traumas, Difficulty trusting, Over-responsibility for others, Difficulty handling feelings, including low self-esteem (shame), and Difficulty giving and receiving love. [90] These are all common core issues in all relationships.

This may be a lot to digest. It is a long song with a lot of angles and descriptions on the theme of being authentic and real in relationships. It comes to us in two levels. We said in the table: it is relationship wisdom disguised as a snappy upbeat romance tune on the surface. As most good poets, the Moodies have been masters at writing lyrics at two or more levels, which we have shown throughout this book. Justin does it again here.

The next song is also multi leveled. John writes a shorter but equally as powerful poem that he and the other four developed into one of their most profound works: 'The Candle of Life.' See what you think.

Table 11.2. Making Meaning of The Candle of Life

by John Lodge 1969 in *TOCCC*

Lyrics	Our Suggested Meaning
Candle Of Life Something you can't hide / Says you're lonely Hidden deep inside / Of you only / It's there for you to see Take a look and be / Burn slowly the candle of life Something there outside / Says we're only / In the hands of time Falling slowly It's there for us to know / With love that we can go Burn slowly the candle of life So love everybody And make them your friend ... Repeat once Repeat S-1 Repeat S-2	We can make meaning here that now we are lonely for something that is missing in our life. We have described it as an emptiness. [87, 90] Our heart feels empty and wants to feel filled. But filled with what? Another person, place or thing to fill the hole in our heart? The main one we can fill ourself with authentically is *us*, our Real Self Hidden deep inside / Of you only and then us *connected* to God. Then it will be easier for us to find healthy relationships with others. The simple words In the hands of time / Falling slowly to us means that we are already and always in the Eternal Now, which is all that there is in time anyway—when we let go of our ego. They repeat the word Love several times throughout this classic.

70

Throughout their music is the base that Love is the answer to most of our problems and conflicts. Other groups have touched on Love, but the Moodies consistently helped us solidify it more within our awareness, which may speak to how they have such an enduring fan base and a long ongoing following.

If you sense another or a different meaning to these two songs above or to any others for which we have offered our interpretation, please consider recording yours on our website specific for this book **MoodiesBook.Wordpress.com**

Another promo photo early on, probably taken in a studio [98]

12 THEIR SOUND

Some 500 years before Christ, the mathematician, scientist and mystic Pythagoras and his fellow Greeks called music the *sonic manifestation of cosmic order*. We and their many fans may see and hear The Moody Blues' music in this light. But, of course, there is a lot more to know about what has made their musical success over the decades, which this book is mostly about. In this and the next chapter we will focus on the main elements of their sound.

Music is simply sound delivered over time. And as you may know from listening to them, it is more. The scholarly *American Standards Association* defines music's essence, *sound* or *timbre* (pronounced *tam*ber) as "... that attribute of sensation in which a listener can judge that two sounds having the same loudness and pitch are different [and that it] depends on the spectrum of the stimulus [and] the waveform, the sound pressure, the frequency location of the spectrum, and the temporal [timing] characteristics of the stimulus." [25, 96]

Although that may be quite a mouthful to us non-academic music lovers, let's look deeper into some of the more detailed characteristics of music as they apply to the Moodies.

THEIR MELODY

Of course, one of the outstanding features of their music is their remarkable *melody*. [2] This word is derived from the Greek *Melos* meaning "tune" and *Oide* meaning "words sung or lyric verse," as in the later term *ode* which refers to song or some recited verse. But how important is it?

Melody is the *single most important aspect* of music, according to many in the field, including music professor Robert Greenberg. [25] In *The New Grove Dictionary of Music and Musicians*, Alexander Ringer, also an internationally acclaimed music professor, wrote that (bear with us for this and the next paragraph, as this definition *does apply* to the Moodies music, which we will get to quickly) "Melody, as defined by *sounds arranged in time* ... represents a *universal human phenomenon* traceable to pre-historic times. ... the broad cultural bases of *logo*genic [word-based] melody are no longer in question." [25]

Ringer continues, summarized by Greenberg: "We are hardwired to make music, to use pitched sounds as a means of communication, and there is a traceable continuum, from an infant's instinctive, preverbal *patho*genic 'musical' communication [the academics' term for preverbal music where pure sound is dominant] to purposeful verbal *logo*genic [where the words or lyrics are dominant] musical communication. These are in contrast to *melo*genic where melody *and* words are equally important, as in opera arias and art song" [25] ['art rock' having been applied sometimes to the Moodies].

What is so powerful here about the Moodies' music is that they are essentially balanced in both of these latter two classical musical areas. For example, '*logo*genic' for their use of Graeme's poems mostly read by Mike, plus the common clarity and power of their lyrics, *and* '*melo*genic' for nearly all their songs wherein they blend their words with their music. Yet, if we play their music mostly in our background sound, we can simply enjoy their sound without focusing on the words. Or when we focus more on the lyrics, because they are so lushly enfolded and enhanced by their music, that we thereby experience their words' taking on even more meaning for us as being a kind of psycho-spiritual nourishment in their sound.

We knew their great voices and rich accompanying instrumental music had special qualities, but until we heard these classical concepts above and below explained, we didn't appreciate them as fully.

LEVELS OF LISTENING ... continued

As you may notice. the longer paragraph above describes another way of going deeper into the levels of listening that we previously introduced in Chapter 9. Now below we expand that chapter some more.

There are two more ways to describe melody that can help us grasp and expand our observational and experiential understanding of their music.

These are specialized music terms that are not commonly used—even among rock and pop musicians, but they do name some key characteristics of the Moodies' music and thereby help us appreciate it more.

Vocal melody means that words tell a story or reflect on an emotional state, *while* their music *so enfolds* them that they *sonically deepen*, *crystallize* and *intensify* their meaning far beyond the power of the words if we read them alone without any background music. [25] Any longtime listener can likely name a few of their favorite Moodies' songs that clearly fit this category. Examples for us include 'Eyes of a Child,' 'Have You Heard,' and 'Out and In.'

Word melody is a melody in which pitches and rhythms are strictly a function of the articulation and rise and fall of the *words* (lyrics) being *sung*. These may be related to both the lead singer *and* the chorus of background Moodies singers. Can you think of examples? To start, we can identify here 'Nights in White Satin,' 'Isn't Life Strange,' and 'One More Time to Live.'

Consider an exercise on their musical building blocks (please allow 20 or more minutes to do this if you have that time): First silently read the lyrics to any of their songs. Then play the song and listen carefully to their vocals—when you *imagine* if they were being sung *acapella*. *Then* listen to the same song in full when combined as a chorus of their blended voices—but now "ignoring" or "blotting out" their instrumental background sounds. *Next* listen again, this time focusing on the *whole piece*, to notice what their instrumental sounds add to the whole. What difference did that make? Could you differentiate these parts? Finally, listen once more for what the *melody* adds.

By first reading and then listening carefully over our long time with their music we have experienced that the *combination* of each of these few ways of naming musical parts does at least four things. It: 1) adds another tangible emotional dimension to their lyric's story, 2) moves the story, 3) keeps us engaged, and 4) makes it more memorable. No wonder that of some 250 bands to appear in the 1960s Birmingham area, that they were the most successful and the most enduring to this day. [2]

About their extraordinary melody, long respected British rock and pop music journalist Keith Altham said, "There is no reason why The Moody Blues should not be talked about in the same breath as The Rolling Stones, The Beatles, Jimi Hendrix and The Who, except that the Moodies made the "cardinal sin" of making melody. [To the Rock and Roll Hall of Fame] ...melody apparently doesn't mix with it [their limited take on R&R]." Some critics don't seem to understand the importance and power of melody.

Mike also called some of their's **counter** melodies, "I was able to wrap these other counter melodies around Justin's vocals and his melodies. Well, what I was really doing, you see, I was the orchestra behind the drums, bass, guitar. So what I was doing... The landscape of it is that I was, you know, the clouds and the blue sky and the sunshine and the rain."

Experienced Moodies' fans and some other readers may find our description of these components of their music to be overdone. Some may not be interested in these more detailed ways of understanding music and how it applies to the Moodies. Even so, we can say more about the elements and quality of their melody, which we continue in the next chapter.

Near airport in France about 1968 [98]

13 THEIR SOUND ...CONTINUED

In the previous chapter we began to describe melody and to outline some of its components and dimensions. The key to good music is making the right sound at the right time. Of course, the Moodies' forte *is* melody—which is sound in time, with the sound being composed of units of notes or pitches of sounds delivered at exactly the right time. When various *pitches* are made *together* to produce a sound-appropriate wave vibration that reaches the delicate tympanic membranes of our ears—*and* in the *right sequence*—we call that *harmony* [25] (Figure 13.1).

Figure 13.1. Relationship between Pitch/Harmony and Melody

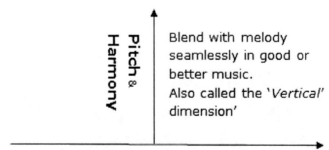

Melody = Pitches & rhythm in Time, also called the '*Horizontal*' dimension

The Moodies' *lyrics* underlie, are supported and enriched by their joint and rich melody and harmony

When we extend enough of the right pitches at the right loudness over time, we call that *melody*. It is all about making the right sound at the right time, in sequence. [25] We also use several related terms to refine our understanding of this process, including meter, rhythm and beat (we briefly summarize these and more musical terms in the **Glossary** in the **Appendix**).

We can summarize the Moodies' three creative components that make up their sound's greatness as consisting of their *lyrics*, *melody* and *harmony*. We can abbreviate these as a simple mnemonic: **L M H**. From our limited understanding of their history, it appears that they made most of their songs in this sequence.

Usually in a moment of creativity, spontaneously or planned, one or two of them wrote the lyrics to a new song. Then they brought them into the studio with the rest of the band and began a second creative process wherein they repeatedly worked out what sounded best to the original lyric authors. Sooner or later they worked on their best harmony for the piece. Sometimes they continued to develop it on stage.

Referring to their harmony, Justin said, "We found that when the four of us – me, John, Ray and Mike sang together, we had a unique vocal sound." No question. We hear it clearly in most of their core 7 songs and many of their later 8. We believe that they rank among the best of harmonic groups, such as the Four Freshmen, the Beach Boys, and David Hykes Harmonic Choir.

Their *signature combination* blends as **L M H**, Lyrics, Melody and Harmony.

TEXTURE

In his 1973 *Rolling Stone* magazine review of *Seventh Sojourn*, Steve Ditlea wrote: "…The major contribution of the British to rock has been their attention to musical texture. … [They] took the multi-layered sound and distinctive effects made possible by modern recording techniques and created textures as palpable as the clothes on your body—and almost as organic." Then he went into some possibly quirky metaphors: "The Kinks are old bleached cotton. Yes sound like carefully crafted brocade, soft and pliant despite the gold threads running through it. Jethro Tull reminds you of brightly died burlap, and T. Rex of silver lamé. And then there's the Moody Blues. The Moodies—they're thick wool tweed in earth colors, lined with shiny grey silk. They're warm but muted on the outside, sensual and smooth within. … On this album as well as their earlier ones, their most satisfying music is also their most tactile, with a variety of rich and flowing textures. Give your intellect a break. *Seventh Sojourn* is music to bask in and feel with your pores as well as your ears."

Texture is another more sophisticated musical term we can use to describe one of the Moodies' many strengths. Texture is the *way* the melodic, rhythmic, and harmonic sounds are *combined*. [25, 75] It includes the *number* and *relationship of* and *among different melodies present* in a section. It is the range or width between lowest and highest pitches according to the number of voices or parts and the relationship between these voices. [25]

Listening to the Moodies as much as we two authors do, which for us is about weekly for an hour or so—we have come to enjoy both their words and music—as though they are one, which they ultimately are.

Claudio Monteverdi, the first great operatic composer, said: "The end of all good music is to affect the soul." Whether we call it their texture or simply their great sound, the Moodies affect on our souls remains a basic reason why we have continued to enjoy them for decades.

In the text and figure 13.1 above we summarized melody as being composed of pitches and rhythm in time. In Chapter 15 below we will expand what we began talking about rhythm. But first let's address a major component of their sound: that previously little-known musical instrument, the Mellotron (spelled with a capital letter or not).

14 THE MELLOTRON

Almost 40 years after their 1970 landmark Isle of Wight Concert, in the documentary film Justin said in retrospect, "The whole thing really changed when we found the Mellotron. Because when I wrote *Nights in White Satin* I came home from a gig one night and just sat on the side of the bed and wrote the basic song. And I took it into the rehearsal room the next day and I played a few bars of it. And the other guys said, 'Yeah, it's all right.' [laughs] And Mike said, 'Play it again.' And I went... And he went... on the Mellotron—and *that's what made it...* the spark that brought it alive." [38]

"It's a sort of strange ethereal sound that had never been really heard before. People weren't used to hearing kind of orchestral sounds coming out of a big stack of amplifiers like that. When you mix the sound of a string section and a brass section, organ and kind of trumpety sound together then it gives this sort of mysterious kind of sound, and the way Mike was able to layer it." [38]

Mike added, "I was able to wrap these other counter melodies around Justin's vocals and his melodies. Well, what I was really doing, you see, I was the orchestra behind the drums, bass, guitar. So what I was doing... The landscape of it is that I was, you know, the clouds and the blue sky and the sunshine and the rain." A perfect poetic description of its sound and Mike's great use of it.

Justin concluded, "It was the Mellotron that really gave us that identity and along with the vocal style that we had and the different characters, elements of the people in it." [38]

The Mellotron came at the right time and was just what Band 2 needed to help them make their great sound and music. The name came from combining MELO(dy) and (elec)TRON(ics). It is a keyboard instrument that plays *any sound* from *other instruments* from prerecorded strips of magnetic tape. Harry Chamberlin invented it in his Wisconsin and then southern California homes in the late 1940s as the 'Chamberlin.' In 1962 his salesman took two to Birmingham, England where Harry and the Bradley brothers of then Bradmatic and later Streetly Electronics formed a subsidiary company named Mellotronics, which developed the first Mellotrons from the Chamberlin. [6, 14, 47, 59] It had three sections: rhythm, accompaniment and lead. It enabled a small band to project a full powerful sound. [6] See online for details on how it works and the many others who used it, at the following website: en.wikipedia.org/wiki/Mellotron.

With his keyboard background, Mike Pinder had "coincidentally" already worked 1 ½ years for Streetly as a quality control and test driver for the Mellotron. He thus became expert at it just in time to use it to significantly enhance the Moodies' core 7 albums sound. But this was not all a simple coincidence, as we elaborate in Chapter 16 on page 97. While many other bands have used it well, none did so with as much precision, power, richness and splendor as Mike and the Moodies did. As we hear almost any song from their core 7 albums, to tell when the Mellotron is active, we have listened carefully with our "mind's ear" to identify and differentiate the guitars, drums, flute and voices. Usually most or all of the *other sounds* we now hear are from the Mellotron. Imagine what the piece would sound like without it, and we can begin to realize how important it has been in enriching the high quality of their music. [47,51]

As an example, in *DoFP* the orchestra and group never actually perform together on the recording. In their songs, the classical instrument sounds we hear were essentially *all* from Pinder's Mellotron. Despite being a lush concept album, it was first made in separate sections, with the band recording each song on their own, which was then given to conductor Peter Knight who quickly composed a suitable "linking" orchestral portion, which the Decca musicians ('London Festival Orchestra') then recorded.

Then in their next album (*ISoaLC*), they chose not to use *any* outside orchestration. All of the classical instrument sounds we hear were and are from the Mellotron. With Mike's keyboard skills, in all nine of their songs and two poems here, they essentially duplicated the full-textured orchestral sound of their first great work DoFP. Three years later, in 'Procession' (to start their 6th album *EGBDF*) they generated *all* of the organ, strings and horns, *plus*

84

the wind, rain, thunder and bird sounds from where you may guess: the Mellotron.

Finally, in 'Legend of a Mind,' among the most engaging, mesmerizing, moving and fun of their musical sequences anywhere is their long *run* in its late middle of where the Mellotron blends in so beautifully with all of their other great instrument sounds. If you have time, take a few minutes and listen to or sample each of these above parts of their work at your leisure. We have experienced 'Legend' in perhaps its purest and clearest form on the 'Isle of Wight' DVD in this great Moodies song.

About Mike's role, Justin said: "The moment we got the Mellotron, everything just kind of opened up a wonderful door to a world of imagination and the landscape of our possibilities. As soon as Mike got it, my songs just seemed to work. Before that, Mike and I were trying to make songs work with the piano as some kind of rock group, which wasn't what we were. Mike was a master. It was a sound effects machine with a few orchestral sounds. He took all the sound effects out and replaced it with duplicates of the orchestral sounds. I think it reached its peak around the time of the Isle of Wight festival that we did in 1970. I still feel his loss and his voice in the band, because he was the prime mover in the whole thing." [4]

As a sidebar, Justin said, "Originally I was the only guy writing with Mike—all of us got behind that material, and everything changed for us. Our audience was suddenly different. People started liking us for the right reasons."

In a late 2012 interview John said that the Mellotron was "... a great breakthrough. When we first started writing material, ages before *Days of Future Passed*, we tried all different keyboards. Mike [was helping] develop it years before, and said why don't we see if it works. It was the perfect instrument for the Moody Blues, because we were only a guitar and bass group with drums. The Mellotron brought everything together. It was difficult to travel with—we ended up buying five of them and leaving them all over the world, so we wouldn't have to travel with them. To handle the parts for it, we went back to one of the original Mellotrons and sampled every instrument and note. It all pretty much plays the same, but there was something different about the Mellotron, probably because it was analog. It's similar to the difference between a vinyl record and a downloaded song." [13]

For a time Mellotrons appeared to be obsolete, as, later on, digital instruments had mostly taken their place. Digital keyboards make similar sounds and are more portable. While digital keyboards have been used since the 1980's to replicate the sounds of many other instruments, they cannot accurately replicate the nuances, idiosyncrasies and special sounds of the Mellotron because of several factors, including its unique sound and the complex physics involved in its tape playback system. This observation and demand from musicians has led to the production of new Mellotrons since 1999. [14, 95]

Of all the disk and tape instruments, the Mellotron has made the strongest comeback. The other related instruments such as the Chamberlin, Orchestron, and Optigan live on as restored original instruments. Each provides unique qualities and variations of sound color as the Mellotron. The Mellotron itself is usually the most available, and due to some unexpected legal shenanigans. the Novatron is now also the exact same instrument. Although the sounds from each instrument are similar, none fully duplicates the other. [6]

The resurgence in the Mellotron and the related tape and disk keyboards has caused a greater appreciation for their place in music history as well as being remarkable examples of mechanical engineering. Their music is on many records now, because musicians and producers still like them, even though there were only about 500 Chamberlins, and 2000 Mellotrons made. The demand for Mellotrons and the others remains into the present and likely on into 21st century. See filmmaker Diana Dilworth's excellent documentary *Mellodrama* for much more. [14, 95]

15 TIME

The important dimension of Time runs throughout their words and music in several important ways, which we refer to in various places throughout this book. We will now address it in more depth here.

Music can be defined as sound *in* and *over* time. We see two levels of time in music: one related to the *mechanics* of the sound in time, and then related to *how* the lyric writers *address time*. We address their mechanics first.

MECHANICS OF TIME IN THEIR MUSIC

We have covered most of the basics of their sound in Chapters 12 through 14 and summarize general music terms in the Glossary in the Appendix. Now we expand what we began talking about *rhythm* in those chapters, at which the Moodies clearly excel.

In music **Rhythm, Beat** and **Tempo** mean about the same. Robert Greenberg defines them as being the shortest division among sounds to which we can execute on an instrument, dance or move. He adds that *tempo* is the *speed* of the beat. We see the Moodies' *rhythm*, *beat* and *tempo* as being at the top in enriching their music and, combined with their usually profound lyrics, outstanding melody, voices and harmony, making them among the best in the history of popular and rock bands.

Music has inherited another useful and related term from the rhythmic element of poetry, which is meter. *Meter* is how the beats are *grouped* in time, how they are grouped in a section of music. They are the *pattern* of lines and accents in the verse of a poem, song, ballad or hymn.

The *sources* of rhythm, beat, and tempo are from *more than* just the percussion section (often abbreviated by many as "drums"). These sources include the rhythms from all of the Moodies' other instruments: guitars, Mellotron, other keyboards, flute, an occasional saxophone, and miscellaneous others, and especially all of their excellent voices.

Justin commented on some of their early creativity using these and more, "By the time we were recording *On The Threshold of a Dream*, we were having every instrument of the orchestra delivered by Decca to the studio. We'd crash around, blow it and pluck it. We got some great sounds out of that stuff ... just ourselves, because we had an hour or two to do it in." [4] And most readers know that they clearly used these to their and our advantage.

One of their unique musical signatures has been to change the beat and texture in the middle of a song, which others and we have called a song-within-a-song. *Examples* include that which we hear in 'Question,' 'Never Comes the Day,' 'Tuesday Afternoon,' and "Legend of a Mind' (which has an *instrumental* one). We see these, of course, as enriching the total song. In 'Eyes of a Child' part

2 they quickened the beat and masterfully enhanced their harmony to such an extent that some have told us of experiencing psychedelic responses hearing it when they were drug free.

We are neither musicians nor music teachers, but we appreciate this crucial component of their melody. Sometimes they extend it into their lyrics. As but one example, in 'English Sunset' they sing to one of their greatest beats with the memorable words 'I feel the *rhythm* of the Earth in my Soul tonight / May it never fade away.' What other examples might you remember?

Figure 15. Graphic of Our Concept of Time

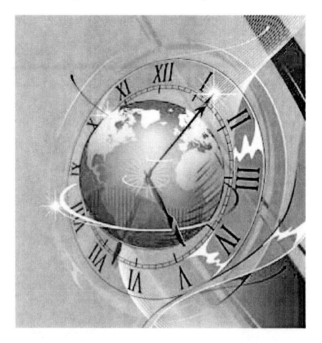

Meaning of Time in Their Lyrics

All music involves time mechanically in these above ways. But it does not always involve meaning.

What is your sense of how often and how important time has been in the Moodies' lyrics? We have seen how sophisticated their use of it has been over their careers. They address time in almost countless ways throughout their words and music. For example, in *Days of Future Passed*—perhaps their most concentrated album involving it—they name the term *directly* as time and also *indirectly* in many and various ways. Examples include: "Day," "Night," "Today," "Yesterday," "Tomorrow," "Now," "Hour," "Awhile," "Morning," "Afternoon," "Twilight time," "Evening," "Years," and "Future."

If interested, consider taking a minute to read through the lyrics of *DoFP* in Chapters 2 and 3 above to see how often they make references to these time-related terms. We could have missed some in our list above.

They also often use time-related metaphors and plays-on-words *such as* in Mike's song 'The Sunset' e.g., "Night has now become / Day for everyone." The album's title *Days of Future Passed* itself doesn't refer to time alone, but takes us first into—and then *beyond*—time, a kind of *meta-time* wherein we are left with the only time there seems to be anyway: the Here and Now. In Chapter 8 above we describe the aftereffects of having a near-death or spiritually transformative experience

(NDE or STE) wherein the experiencers talk often about how their prior concepts of time have changed for them. Near-death experiencers afterwards tend not to relate to our conventional default mode of linear time, but tend to enjoy the Here and Now more often.

None of their other core 7 album titles refers directly to time, but many of their *songs* and Graeme's *poems* within them do so repeatedly. For example, in 'Ride my Seesaw' we hear *run for time*, in 'House of Four Doors' *forever,* and 'Legend of a Mind' we hear *brings you back the same day*.

How we experience time is effected by how we perceive reality. Two definitions: time is *what clocks measure* (Figure 15 above) and, almost tongue-in-cheek, time is *what keeps everything from happening at once*. Some see time as part of the fundamental structure of the universe—a dimension independent of events, in which events occur in sequence, sometimes called Newtonian time. The opposing view is that time does not refer to any kind of "container" that events and objects "move through," nor to any entity that "flows," but that it is instead part of a fundamental intellectual structure (together with space and number) within which we sequence and compare events. Thus, time is neither an event nor a thing, and thereby is not itself measurable, nor can it be travelled. [78]

We can use time to define other things from the speed of various objects to the space-time continuum (briefly defined as the usual three dimensions but then interacting with time as a fourth dimension). [78]

TIME AND ALTERED STATES OF CONSCIOUSNESS

Time usually varies in altered states of consciousness (ASCs) from most causes. [74] For example, it can and often does appear to slow in our *perception* when using cannabis, depending on the potency of the particular lot used, and with psychedelics it *usually* slows in varying degrees. Cannabis has been used often enough by countless Moodies' fans, who have said that it intensifies their experience of appreciating and enjoying their words and music. Yet it is not at all a requirement for such enjoyment enhancement.

By contrast, stimulants such as nicotine, caffeine, cocaine and amphetamines speed up our perception of time, making users feel as though time is passing more quickly. [29] A few fans may have used one or more of these stimulants to try to enhance our experience of their music. Not us.

Probably as many if not *more* of us *most often* enjoy their music drug free. In fact the verbal/intellectual and auditory quality of their combined words and music alone are plenty to induce a *natural* ASC. They put us into the Now with regularity, of which they frequently remind us. They have repeatedly helped us remember the importance of living in the Now with their strong message. When we focus on their music or are working on a project with it playing in the background, we can sometimes enter into what psychologist Mike Csikszentmihalyi calls the *flow state*, where time slows or even seems to stand still for us. Flow is the feeling experience of *energized focus* in a task or activity where we are fully involved, immersed, and successful in the process of the activity. It is an ideal feeling state for us when we are our most creative. He has documented this joyful feeling across several areas of our life. [12]

We believe that one of many reasons why the Moodies have succeeded over the decades is that— no matter whether they go into the studio to record or they are on tour performing in front of us—they know how to so focus that they are essentially always in a flow state of energized focus. They are also nearly always getting our appropriate appreciation, adoration and love that we project back onto them throughout their performance, strengthening their flow state experience.

One common aftereffect for people who have had a spiritually transformative experience is a shift in the way they experience time. It doesn't matter if it's drug induced or happens near death or by another way, and we may eventually discover somewhere along the way that there is no linear time in Eternity. There is only Now. Listening to the Moodies' words and music reminds us of that "timeless" realization.

16 BACK TO THEIR FUTURE'S PAST

With a play-on-words on their classic album *Days of Future Passed* as this chapter's title, let's look deeper at some interesting and a few even remarkable observations on how the group came together and developed their words and music.

Their earliest history may have been a bit disjointed, but as we show in the *Timeline* in the **Appendix**, that seemingly jumbled series of events was apparently just what they needed to become the artists and band that they did. To make this chapter's flow clearer, take a minute and read the Timeline's first page.

Their beginnings evolved over a ten year gestational period of being first inspired, interested and finally involved in writing, developing, rehearsing and performing their music. Scholars on creativity describe the *'Ten-year rule,'* which shows that, on average, it requires about a decade of intense study and practice to acquire world-class expertise in most domains of achievement. [67] Data suggest that a person needs about ten years of work, or ten thousand hours (about 3.8 hours a day for ten years), to be invested into a knowledge-based skill for expertise to develop. As individuals and as a group, the Moodies took at least 10 years from the mid-to-late 1950s to 1967 to begin to acquire their creative musical expertise.

We know that learning music skills takes a lot of dedication and practice, which they each did from a young age. Mike developed his musical abilities from toddlerhood, Justin from age 8, John soon after that, and Ray and Graeme from their early teen years. The first two had their parents' strong support and encouragement. By their late teens they were all budding into being serious musicians. But something remarkable happened during the last two of this ten year developmental period. To understand that process we describe a key related term.

Synchronicity is a *meaningful coincidence*. It is the experience of two or more simultaneous or near simultaneous events that are apparently causally unrelated or unlikely to occur together by chance, yet they are experienced as occurring together in a meaningful manner. The odd events, because of their occurrence so close in time, are instilled with meaning by those who recognize them as so. [58] Here is what we found:

It is remarkable that the Moody Blues survived out of some 250 R&B groups that developed in the Birmingham area in the 1960s. How did that happen? From 1965 to 1967 a series of some twelve *synchronicities* or important steps happened. These otherwise seemingly separate occurrences happened to, with, from and for them, which then set the stage for them to create their new and then vastly improved and, soon, highly successful music.

Were these random events? These twelve events—and their unexpected sequence and flow—appear to have been so crucial that if any one and certainly if more of them had *not* happened, we may likely not have the quality of their music as we know it today. Here is our and others' understanding about how and why this special sequence of happenings came about and what it may mean for us as listeners and fans. Please study these twelve synchronistic events that had a major impact on their music. *In review*: Their timing, occurrence, flow and ultimate results are remarkable and key to bringing about the band as we have known it. Take your time looking at each.

Table 16. Twelve Synchronicities that Had a Major Impact on Their Music

1) In July and October 1966 Denny Laine and Clint Warwick respectively and respectfully leave Band 1.

2) Mike Pinder develops his and their use of the *Mellotron* that itself was developed and made in 1963 in the Birmingham area. They could not afford a new one, but Mike found one used under some trash in a Dunlop Tire employee's club for £80.

3) Later in 1966, they hire John Lodge and, also synchronistically, find and hire Justin Hayward in about December.

4) From 1966 to 67 they all continue struggling to survive musically and financially.

5) A local British man seriously criticizes a recent performance. Driving home in 1966, they quickly agree and decide to change.

6) They stop all their previous music, dress, and performance.

7) A Belgian club owner offers them his space and venue to begin their new creativity and work, which they do.

8) Get a call from a Paris venue and become a local musical success.

9) September 1967 get a call from Decca about making a trial album re Dvorak symphony. They prefer to develop their own stage show and receive support from Decca executive Hugh Mendl, producer Tony Clark, sound engineer Derek Varnals and orchestra composer and leader Peter Knight.

10) A Decca studio happens to be free for three weeks, but prior had prepared only 'Dawn is a Feeling' and 'Nights in White Satin'

11) They work intensely for three weeks to write and develop the six other songs and two poems for *Days of Future Passed.*

12) Decca executives are skeptical to publish it, but American Decca/London executive Walt McGuire likes, backs and promotes it. What would have happened if he had not done so?

Reading over this list and connecting each seemingly isolated event with the next, we can see this sequence as one meaningful coincidence after another. These synchronicities brought together a group of musicians that focused on something important and non-physical that changed their prior ways of writing, composing and performing. In varying degrees, their lyrics and music also changed the lives of countless people who have listened to them now for nearly 50 years.

This now clear sequence of events gave way to the Moodies' new creative style that broke all their old roles, rules and habits. They continued to evolve with new forms and patterns wherein they wrapped their words and messages in far more captivating melodies that made significant creative advances.

Through the chain of their music they gently draw us the listener in and teach us the deeper meanings of relationships, romance and beyond into mature love and natural spirituality. They made a whole new field that blended classical, pop and rock to inspire us to reach beyond our ordinary conscious mind to transcend that 'small r' or default reality, thereby reminding or waking us up to the bigger Reality. Continuing to take their music in with our open ears, eyes and heart, is to become awakened to a spirituality that directly connects us and may at times transcend conventional religion.

They transmit a mystical (soul nourishing) message that is highlighted by the experience of their distinctive melody enfolding their spiritually evolved lyrics. As we listen, we may transcend our ordinary life and become absorbed in their creativity, fantasy and the magic, *yet reality*, of their words and music. What we read in their lyrics and hear as they sing and express with their instruments is the manifestation of an intention to transcend the limitations of our otherwise limited life.

There is still more to their story, evolution and current members and setting, which we continue in the next chapter.

17 Their Future's Past ...continued

Music journalist Lee Zimmerman said, "Who The Moody Blues became qualified them as one of Britain's most imaginative ensembles, one whose penchant for creative concepts and psychedelic sensibilities began with *Days of Future Passed*, an album that ranks alongside *Sgt. Pepper*, *In the Court of the Crimson King*, *Tommy* and other game-changing standard bearers of late 1960s British rock." [97] Although it was too brief, that summarized their work as a group. But what can we say about them as individual artists?

Their diversity was a strength. In 1984 *Higher & Higher* magazine co-editor Mark Moerman said what savvy fans knew, "The creative process of the group was a product of the collaborate efforts of five people, with none of them standing out as a group leader or star." Justin said, "Every Moody is a very different personality and has a very different role to fulfill within the band. The reason it works is because we are five very different people. ... It's the combination that makes the whole thing work." We summarize a bare capsule of what we have found about them and their works in Table 17.1. [50]

About their preferences in writing their lyrics, Justin said, "For Mike and I, it was almost like school. I had to have everything done before I went into the studio. ... For John, Ray and Graeme, because they hadn't been writers before, [they]

Table 17.1. Members' Works *Capsule* Summary

Member	Summary of Works
All Five	All creative and different. Their differentness was a strength in writing and making their music.
Michael Thomas Pinder	'Resident mystic' Musician since 3 years-old. Long time spiritual seeker, reflected in essentially all of his 19 songs with the MBs. He read all core 7 poems but one.
Ray Thomas	Fanciful, whimsical and often some deeper songs. Musician and singer since teen years. Self-taught flautist. To most of their songs Ray added great flute components. Grand Welsh voice.
Graeme Edge	'Poet' with good spiritual direction. Mother a pianist, father and grandfather music hall singers. Learned drums self-taught just before he joined Mike and Ray. [72]
John Charles Lodge	All-around. Rocker. Musician from young age. Bass, acoustic guitar, cello, voice. Wrote lyrics that varied from relationship (e.g., 'Eyes of a Child') to mystical to rock.
David Justin Hayward	Romantic, Folk. Musician from age 9. Lead guitar, sitar, vocals. Kept band together. June Price wrote: "... beneath his soft-spoken and thoughtful manner is the quiet dignity and strength that has taken the Moody Blues to the top again and again. He is the person most likely to argue against his individual importance." [63]

came at it differently. They let things happen in the studio and then worked on them. ... I loved working on Ray's stuff, because I could just make up the chords. I'd say, 'What about this?' and he'd say, 'That sounds great!' I could have said a completely different chord and he'd say, 'That sounds great!' That was the beauty of it. We all came from a different starting point. Mike was a fantastic pub pianist. He could sit there and entertain people for hours. I came from folk clubs and constructing songs for publishing. The others came at it from a completely different point of view, and that's what made the whole thing interesting. Each one of us had different things to bring to an album." [4]

THEIR AGES ALONG THE WAY

To our knowledge no one has chronicled their ages over the time of their early works, which we summarize in Table 17.2 below. They were in their 20s when they made their core 7.

THEIR MUSICIANS OVER TIME

Although the general line-up of the Moody Blues has been relatively stable since 1978, there have been some replacements with hired musicians from then until to today. Over the recent decades the three core members (JH, JL, GE) have maintained or improved their sound and stage delivery. Today they have four hired musicians performing with them, for a total of seven, as we show in the tables below.

Table 17.2. Ages of Members over their Early Time

Time → B'day Year ↓	Age in early bands 1958	Band 1 1964	Band 2 1966	DoFP album 1967	Seventh Sojourn 1972	Age in 2013
Mike Pinder 1941	17 years -old	23	24	25	30	71
Ray Thomas 1941						
Graeme Edge 1941						
John Lodge 1942 or 3	15 * (not in one)	21	23	24	29	69
Justin Hayward 1946	12 (not in one)	18	20	20	25	67

*At 15 John was temporarily with Mike and Ray in their R&B band 'El Riot & the Rebels'.

The most musicians on stage at one time with them was twelve, from 1990 to 2001.

Table 17.3. Performers over the Decades from 1964

Began	Name	Contribution	Left Band
1964	**Mike Pinder**	keyboards, vocals with RT were 1st 2 founders	1978
	Ray Thomas	vocals, flute, percussion, 1996 added harmonica	late 2002
	Graeme Edge ●	drums, percussion	Still active
	Denny Laine Clint Warwick	guitar, vocals bass, vocals	1965

1965	Rodney Clark	bass, vocals	
Late 1965	**John •** **Lodge**	bass, guitar, vocals	Still active
1966	**Justin•** **Hayward**	guitar, vocals	Still active
1978	Patrick Moraz	keyboards (takes Pinder's place on tour and recording)	Left 1991
1986	Bias Boshell	Keyboards (rejoined 1989)	2001
1987	Guy Allison	keyboards	1990
1986	Janis Liebhart Wendy McKenzie	backing vocals	1987
1988	Shaun Murphy Naomi Starr	backing vocals	1990
1990	Paul Bliss •	keyboards, guitar	
	Bekka Bramlett Terry Wood	backing vocals	
1991	Gordon Marshall •	drums, percussion	
1991	June Boyce Susan Shattock	backing vocals	1993 2000
1993	Tracy Graham	backing vocals	2001
2002	Norda Mullen •	flute, guitar, percussion, vocals	
	Bernie Barlow •	keyboards, percussion, vocals (3 year leave '06-9)	
2006	Julie Ragins	keyboards, percussion, vocals	2009

• = Current group. All original 5 wrote, composed and performed

We detail their outstanding musicians *by year* in Table 17.4 below. Note that each block of years reads from top to bottom, so turn the page to follow them easier *by column*, and not by row.

Table 17.4. More Detailed Performers Listed by Years

1964 - 1966	2001 - 2002
Mike Pinder - keyboards, vocals	Justin Hayward
Ray Thomas - vocals, flute,	John Lodge
percussion	Ray Thomas
Denny Laine - guitar, vocals	Graeme Edge
Clint Warwick - bass, vocals	with
Graeme Edge - drums, percussion	Paul Bliss
Rodney Clark - bass, vocals	Bernie Barlow - keyboards,
	percussion, vocals
	Gordon Marshall
1966 - 1978	**2002 - 2006**
Justin Hayward	Justin Hayward
John Lodge	John Lodge
Ray Thomas - add harmonica	Graeme Edge
Mike Pinder	with
Graeme Edge - add vocals	*Add* Norda Mullen - flute, guitar,
	percussion, vocals
	Paul Bliss
	Bernie Barlow
	Gordon Marshall
1978 - 1986	**2002 - 2006**
Justin Hayward	Justin Hayward
John Lodge	John Lodge
Ray Thomas – add percussion,	Graeme Edge
Graeme Edge	with
	Norda Mullen -add percussion,
Patrick Moraz – *new* keyboards	Paul Bliss
	Bernie Barlow - keyboards,
	percussion, vocals
	Gordon Marshall
1986 - 1990	**2006 - 2009**
Justin Hayward	Justin Hayward
John Lodge	John Lodge
Ray Thomas	Graeme Edge, with
Graeme Edge	Norda Mullen add harmonica
Patrick Moraz - add some vocals	Paul Bliss
with	Gordon Marshall
Bias Boshell -keyboards(1986)	Julie Ragins - keyboards,
Guy Allison - keyboards(1987-	percussion, vocals
1990)	(Barlow on leave)

Janis Liebhart – all below were backing vocals (1986-1987) Wendy McKenzie -(1986-1987) Shaun Murphy - (1988-1990) Naomi Starr - (1988-1990)	
1990 - 2001 Justin Hayward John Lodge Ray Thomas Graeme Edge with Bias Boshell - keyboards Paul Bliss - keyboards, guitar Gordon Marshall - drums, percussion (joined in 1991) and Bekka Bramlett – plus all below were backing vocals (1990) Terry Wood (1990) June Boyce (1991-1993) Susan Shattock (1991-2000) Tracy Graham (1993-2001)	**2009 - present** Justin Hayward John Lodge Graeme Edge with Norda Mullen - flute, guitar, percussion, harmonica, vocals Paul Bliss - keyboards, guitar Gordon Marshall Bernie Barlow returns At times late 2012 Julie Ragins - keyboards, percussion, vocals (Barlow on leave) At times late 2012 Alan Hewitt – keyboards e.g., in Mesa, AZ concert

We did not use the word *outstanding* above lightly in referring to their many hired musicians. We called them so because it speaks to the original band members' ability and attention to pick quality new people who can and do maintain their great sound on their ongoing tour concerts. Their current four additional musicians have blended well, with flautist Norda Mullen, second drummer Gordy Marshall, keyboardist Paul Bliss, and Bernie Barlow or Julie Ragins' vocals and keyboards.

They still don't seem to miss a beat.

Mike Pinder Departs

Their core 7 albums of course had compositions from all of the original five, but in 1978 their members began to change over time. Many fans and some critics believe that Mike Pinder's leaving that year was a major loss in several important ways. Mike had clearly added several strengths to the band: 1) he wrote 19 of their songs, 2) was in a sense their "Resident mystic" (which greatly strengthened their appeal to many of us spiritually inclined), 3) had a great speaking voice to read most of Graeme's poems to start and end each of their core 7 albums, 4) had a very good singing voice, and maybe most of all 5) brought the classical and rich, mystical sound of the Mellotron to essentially all of their core 7 albums' songs. (See 5 pages below for more and how his leaving interacted with other factors on the changes in their later music after their core 7.)

In the next chapter we continue commenting on their core 7 and then finish with comments and other information on their work.

18 THEIR FUTURE'S PAST ...CONCLUDED

In this chapter we continue first with some more selected comments and interesting information on their classic or core 7 albums. Then we summarize what some reviewers and fans have written about their later words and music, after 1972.

Over the past nearly 50 years in their comments most fans and critics have focused on their core 7 albums. Why? After their three to five- (when counting touring) -year hiatus, they made *eight* more albums. These included *Octave* (in 1978), *Long Distance Voyager* (1981), *The Present* (1988), *The Other Side of Life* (1986), *Sur la Mer* (1988), *Keys of the Kingdom* (1991), *Strange Times* (1999), and finally *December* (2003).

Since 1978 many of us have said that we were continuously waiting for one of these to match the overall quality of any of one their core 7. Did that ever happen? Was it even possible? What was so unique about their core 7 albums that could have prohibited such a continuation or match? To answer that key question that so many may have asked themselves privately in their thoughts or in an informal conversation with others—or for the rare fan or reviewer who published their writing about it, doing that would take up more space than we have here, even as we may have accomplished even minimally over the rest of this book. Before we address these questions about the above eight albums, it may be useful first to review some notes on their core 7, even if we look at only a few of their seemingly surface aspects. Look over the table below. If any of it does not interest you, skip on to the next section on their *post* core 7 works.

Table 18.1. Core 7 Albums' Various and Interesting Notes

Title/date charts	Notes
DoFP **1967** 11 Nov *Examples reached* : No. 27 on UK album; 5 yrs later was # 3 on Billboard 200 in USA	Your favorite? Depends. In which genre you may describe it, clearly a classic. Though Decca was ecstatic with the sales results, including its singles, assigning Clarke & Varnals ongoing to work with them, they dropped formal orchestra from next album *Lost Chord*. Having just paid *its* debt & wanting more musical creativity, the band also chose not to use or finance one. [17] In 1993 NASA chief astronaut Robert Gibson gave the Moodies a plaque documenting that on every outer-stratospheric mission the astronauts heard *Days* and *Seventh Sojourn*. Yet another example of being space (their sound went with them over 10 million miles) and time travelers. [80]
ISoLC **1968** No. 5 on UK album # 23 on Billboard 200 USA	More mystical than *Days*. Inspired by 1945 Jimmy Durante song "I'm the guy who found the lost chord." The lost chord may well be "Om" (ōm, aum, aaaooouuumm; a universal mantra) the album's last song, also recognized by mystics and many spiritual seekers as a sound of pure consciousness. Used no orchestra but their own instruments and the Mellotron—which was major in its signature sound. [19]
OtToaD **1969** 1 UK 20 BB 200 2 RPM Canada	Their *first chart-topping* LP in England, on the charts for an astonishing 70 weeks. [19] Explores dreams and more. Begins with a poem with electronic sounds which also finish the album; LP editions were pressed to continue these sounds into the

	album's run-out groove, causing them to play continuously until tone-arm lifted. Tape and CD versions end with these sounds slowly faded out.
TOCCC 1969 2 in UK 14 USA	Others' and our favorite. A concept album inspired by the first moon landing, with themes of space travel and children. "Thinking man's rock. ... near perfect, turn off the lights, close your eyes and let the music take you. It's that haunting. Their most mature, fully realized effort to date, arguably surpassing even the milestone DoFP in its elegance and vision. They were always capable of both songcraft and experimentalism, but this was the first time they combined them both successfully." [79] First album released on their newly-formed *Threshold Records* label for Decca distribution, named after their previous album.
AQoB 1970 No.1 in UK 3 in USA	Some critics loved it, as did many of us. [48] For this they decreased their prior heavier overdubbing to make it easier to perform their songs in concert. The 1997 remastered edition brings out the guitar sound with force and clarity, and the sleeve notes address the turmoil they were starting to feel after three years of such success. No lyrics included on sleeve, but all their words are widely available online and on older sleeves.
EGBDF 1971 1 UK alb 2 BB200	The opening 'Procession,' only one written by all five, was a review of the history of music from the beginning to then: desolation, creation, and communication, then used again along with 18 other -ation/-ion words in their 6th gloriously memorable John Lodge piece 'One More Time to Live.' In 1971 Stu Werbin of Rolling Stone magazine called this song the album's most powerful and intricate, although several others were excellent. The title is taken from the student mnemonic for the lines of the treble clef: E-G-B-D-F. These notes are heard played on piano during 'Procession.' First album not promoted by any singles. The cover of this book is an oil copy by CW of its cover art.

SS Released in late 1972 5 UK 1 USA for 5 weeks	Recorded in Mike's home studio due to a fire in an LA studio. Mike added the Chamberlin, which simulated orchestral sounds more realistically and easily than the Mellotron. John said, 'I'm Just a Singer in a R&R Band' was his response to fans who mistakenly read guru-like wisdom into their often philosophical lyrics, saying they were just as worried by the crises of the modern world and have just as few answers as everyone. But they also *asked important questions* and raised important *relationship issues so well*, as we show throughout this book. And with these 8 songs they only strengthen their ongoing psycho-spiritual message and maintain their high consciousness. Bruce Eder called it "their last wholly successful record," although as we know they were not about to stop making music." [Eder]

THEIR NEXT EIGHT, OR POST CORE-7

This was the hardest section in this book for us to write. From 1978 and beyond others and we have thought that unfortunately, for these eight post core 7 albums, much of their magic was gone. [73] (Most savvy readers will know what we mean by 'magic' here, and it is not sleight-of-hand.) We had all hoped and expected that it would continue. Yet, not all of it was gone. These talented, creative, dedicated and hard working musicians found themselves now in a different time and a new musical era and another cultural time.

The 1980s turned out to be one of the worst times for them to make their previously sophisticated music—with several factors interacting: 1) punk, disco and over-synth now predominating, they lost their momentum of the 60s. And they were not the same group as their prior starting five. 2) Except for his 'One Step into the Light' in *Octave*, they lost Mike's powerful contributions. 3) They included Ray less often on these albums. 4) Patrick Moraz' synth sounds so often overdone. [46, 73] 5) In 1986 they hired a new producer Tony Visconti who was a kind of double-edged sword. He "overly-popped" them— while *a few* new songs (one or occasionally two on each new album) became a hit with a new generation now growing up and who apparently may have had less psycho-spiritual taste. By contrast, perhaps surprising to some, Justin said, "The greatest thing that happened after that—for me—was Tony Visconti. To have hit records again in the '80s—to be on MTV and all of that kind of stuff when you're 40—is just fantastic! I could actually look at it, not be stoned and enjoy it, which was wonderful." [4]

6) Another and major loss was their great core 7 producer Tony Clarke, who had to drop out in the middle of their making *Octave*. Mike Pinder said, "Tony is rarely given enough credit for his contribution to the music, not only in the studio production but as our trusted friend. He had a great wit and musical ear for what we wanted and needed. He contributed countless creative ideas in developing our songs. Once Ray, John, Graeme, Justin or I had a song ready, we would all add improvements to the arrangement or the sonic effects. His ideas are intertwined in all the Core 7 albums and he added as many as anyone. Plus,

Tony was a gentle man, very intelligent with a great sense of humor. He truly was the sixth Moody."

Yet as shown by a few positive factors, including ongoing album sales and so many to mostly sold-out concerts to this day, they have continued to thrive.

In their new material there were a few clear highlights that many of us have enjoyed (you pick your favorites, and we have ours). With all these changes they persisted and created something new. They continued making some good to *occasionally* superior music, given the culture, times and musicians that they still had. They had, perhaps again, synchronistically found a new level of creativity in some to many of their new songs that many have enjoyed over the years. And, as we note in the title of this book, their message remains timeless.

We are still entranced when we watch their concerts on DVD performing selected of their core 7 songs and several from their later 8. When Ray Thomas retired, we saw a similar thing happen again. In March 2012 at Atlanta's Fox Theatre we saw the three current Moodies perform with a full crowd that gave them a standing ovation at the end. They have survived many changes and continue to bounce back and repeatedly thrive.

Let's start with **Octave**: Reviewers and one-time-fans Andrew and Shawn Dow summarize their responses on their website, with a warning. [16] They start their critiques with *Octave* (and if time, please look at their website and see what you think): "This has to be the longest album in history! ... They don't sound like the Moody Blues, they sound like 5 guys that did solo projects, giving us a taste of what they did on their break from the band, returning in an era of punk music and disco.

" ... [Yet it] was a massive seller in the classic comeback sense. *Octave* went double platinum in Canada and 'Driftwood' became a mega-hit. 'Steppin' In Slide Zone' was a hit, but not to as great a degree. ... Another Moody Blues historical non-classic album ...hard to sit through and take seriously, although there are moments that shine through ... ." [16]

We wish we had enough space on these pages to cover all of these eight albums to this degree. Several critics and critic-fans do cover them in great detail, many with multiple fan comments. We have enjoyed reading for example, the detailed websites of many: • John McFerrin • *ProgArchives* • Mark's (Prindle) reviews • Don Ignacio • MBs Fan Anthology • *Our Moodies website* → for your feedback on this book • George Starotsin and • Bruce Eder (he has no single website like the above, so we have had to search for his many reviews). Please see the **Appendix** section just before the References for their web addresses.

With this brief background, let's look at some aspects of their post-core 7 albums, which we summarize in the table below.

Table 18.1. Their Later Eight Albums:
→ **Various and Interesting Notes**

Title/date charts	Notes
Octave **1978** *Examples reached* : Billboard 13 UK album 6 Double platinum in Canada *Singles* -Slide Zone BB Hot 100 39 -Driftwood BB Hot 100 69 (Singles not shown on other albums here)	Many fans were disappointed. [16, 73, Eder] Or were you moved by any of it? *Tracks* - Steppin' In a Slide Zone, Under Moonshine, Had to Fall in Love, I'll Be Level With You, Driftwood, Top Rank Suite, I'm Your Man, Survival, One Step Into the Light, The Day We Meet Again. Some said it was a good comeback. [Eder] • Reviewer-fan George Starotsin wrote, "...despite all the complaints, the album is not THAT bad - at least, not as awful as some fans often describe it. ... [while] they're rather well-written, they just lack any kind of spark. The magic is gone." [73] • Mike had one good song 'One Step Into the Light'—a kind of ending to his MB career, otherwise little input or Mellotron, or Ray's flute. In the middle of the sessions their great producer Tony Clarke (the '6th Moodie') had to leave. [46] Last track 'Day We Meet Again' is a beautiful anthem about the sorrow of saying goodbye (not to mention that it's dedicated to Mike). "Driftwood" is one of Justin's best. [46]
Long **Distance** **Voyager** **1981** No. 1 Canada, 1 in USA BB UK 7 NZ 8 Europe 12 - 46	Any you like? *Songs*- The Voice, Talking Out of Turn, Gemini Dream, In My World, Meanwhile, 22,000 Days, Nervous, Painted Smile, Reflective Smile, Veteran Cosmic Rocker. '• The Voice' "...greatest melody on the album, and Hayward shines as a vocalist again." [73] • *ProgArchives* critic *Gatot* said, "[there is] something missing ... nothing that stirs my emotions ... barely nice melody ... only suitable for those big fans of The

	Moody Blues or the Collectors." • "...only track close to bad is the purely disco 'Gemini Dream.' ... Pinder's mellotron made the Moodie's sound. Moraz' synths sounded like everybody else's in the 80's." [46]
The Present 1983 26 BB 200	Any here? *Songs-* Blue World, Meet Me Halfway, Sitting at the Wheel, Going Nowhere, Hole In The World, Under My Feet, It's Cold Outside of Your Heart, Running Water, I Am, Sorry. • John McFerrin "...traces of 'rock' are completely gone, replaced with a solid mixture of various pop elements." [46] Some nice ballads, but still missing it.
Other Side of Life 1986 24 in UK albs 9 BB 200 USA	How about these? Songs- Your Wildest Dreams, Talkin' Talkin', Rock 'N' Roll Over You, I Just Don't Care, Running Out of Love, The Other Side of Life, The Spirit, Slings and Arrows, It May be a Fire. [Eder] Took on new producer *Tony Visconti* and some said their sound got even worse. • McFerrin: "...some solid music ... [but] most is completely disposable ... this is 1986 we're talking about. Don't be afraid to buy it, [but only] *if* you're a *big fan.* [79]
Sur La Mer 1988 No.1 in UK briefly 38 BB 200 in USA	We like this one: 'I Know You're Out There Somewhere' *The rest*: Want to be With You, River of Endless Love, No More Lies, Here Comes The Weekend, Vintage Wine, Breaking Point, Miracle, Love is on the Run, Deep. • Starotsin said, " ...the 80s ... They had a contract... had to be marketed, ...sound stylish and 'cool' (...a horrendous word when applied to the worst musical decade in history) ...written exclusively by Hayward and Lodge, with the other two out of the studio. ... I think Moraz' ... synth noises or not, *Sur La Mer* couldn't have turned out otherwise." [73]
Keys of the Kingdom 1991	Any you like? *Songs-* **Say It With Love,** Bless the Wings (That Bring You Back), Is This Heaven?, **Say What You Mean** (Parts 1 & 2), Lean on Me (Tonight), Hope and Pray, Shadows on The Wall, Once is Enough,

54 UK alb **94 BB 200**	Celtic Sonant, Magic, Never Blame the Rainbows for the Rain [46] • The **bolded** pieces above we analyze in the chapters above. • *ProgArchives*: gives it 2 stars "[Much] is predictable and meaningless, showing a band which sells its soul to be aired on the radio. But ... some fine ideas shine through, particularly in ... their melody and production." • Some pieces produced by Tony Visconti are thankfully his last with them.
Strange Times 1999 **92 UK alb** **93 BB200**	Any you like? Songs - English Sunset, Haunted, Sooner or Later, Wherever You Are, Foolish Love, Love Don't Come Easy, All That Is Real Is You, Strange Times, Words You Say, My Little Lovely, Forever Now, The One, The Swallow, Nothing Changes. *Listen and decide*: • McFerrin: "...their take on aging and the passage of time. ...terrific pair of "English Sunset" and "Haunted." [46] • Starotsin: "... kinda shallow...[yet] ... among Lodge's best ever written."
December 2003	Songs - Don't Need A Reindeer, December Snow, In the Quiet of Christmas Morning, On This Christmas Day, Happy Xmas (War Is Over), A Winter's Tale, The Spirit of Christmas, Yes I Believe, When a Child Is Born, White Christmas, In The Bleak Midwinter. • McFerrin: "...don't ignore it forever if you're a Moodies diehard." • December is not the first album Ray Thomas wasn't on. He was not on the 2 Tony Visconti produced albums in 86 and 88. He is listed as being on the albums because he was still a member of the Moody Blues. Also, a drum machine was used on one of those two albums so Graeme isn't on one of them either.

These above were eight albums with some similarities among them and affected by a lot of changes over time in the background as they wrote

117

and released them, as we detailed and described on pages 111-112 above.

The above has been but a small sample of what we found listening to these albums over the past decades and reading these many and great fan and critics reactions. Please read our 'Fan and Reviewer Websites' in the Appendix below just before the Reference section if you want to see more good reviewer comments.

19   SPIRITUALITY - STAGE 3 HEALING

Stage 3 healing is about realizing and integrating spirituality into our life. It involves our authentic relationship with our self, others and God.

Spirituality takes us deeper into these basic three relationships. In it we regularly ask such perennial questions as: Who am I? What am I doing here? Where am I going? and How can I get any peace?

Spiritual practices, including meditation, prayer and contemplation help us become more aware of our inner life, which the Moodies have repeatedly addressed and done so more clearly than most other bands. Spiritual experiences include having a *felt connection* to a Larger Reality or God, which Twelve Step fellowship members call 'the God of our understanding' or Higher Power. Spiritual practices also include experiencing a more developed and integrated Real Self, joining with healthy others at a higher and healthier level, and frequently with nature. Becoming more aware of these aspects, and more, of our spirituality usually inspires and enriches our life.

We see the Moodies' strength as being in their writing, developing together, singing and making great music that *involves spirituality* in several dimensions. This deep and meaningful aspect of their music is what we believe makes up a large part of the reason why so many of us have continued to listen to and enjoy hearing them for almost fifty years now. In the following sections we offer several examples of the power of their spirituality.

THE LAND OF MAKE-BELIEVE

Good poetry is so concentrated and economical that it makes us think, and the best moves us. With good poetry's brevity, meter and metaphor it puts us in a trance wherein we can go into our unconscious mind and thereby ideally access and at times resolve some of our unfinished business. Justin's poetic lyrics below do just that in five short stanzas. Let's take a look at it in Table 19.1 below.

Table 19.1. Making Meaning of The Land of Make-Believe
by Justin Hayward from *Seventh Sojourn* 1972

Lyrics	Our Suggested Meaning
The Land of Make-Believe We're living in a land of make-believe And trying not to let it show Maybe in that land of make-believe Heartaches can turn into joy	The 'land of make-believe' is the false self/ego's world of constantly creating drama because it has to be always right and in control. But our Real Self (Child Within/'Eyes of a Child') lives in 'Realville,' also known as God's World of Love and joy—as they sing.
We're breathing in the smoke of high and low / We're taking up a lot of room/ Somewhere in the dark and silent night	This is the 'it' that we are trying to conceal (trying not to let **it** show). Finding ourself in these two worlds leaves us in a duality wherein the ego's world *seems* real, but is actually not, since only Love's /God's World is real. [88, 89]

Our prayer will be heard, Make it soon So fly little bird / Up into the clear blue sky And carry the word Love's the only reason why, why Open all the shutters on your windows Unlock all the locks upon your doors Brush away the cobwebs from your daydreams No secrets come between us anymore Oh, say it's true Only love will see you through You know what love can do to you	By 'breathing in the smoke of high and low' we let ourself buy into the duality of the ego's drama, which takes up a lot of our time and energy ('...a lot of room'). [88, 89] When we awaken to this dynamic and even *pray* about it, we may then '...fly little bird / Up into the clear blue sky / And carry the word / Love's the only reason why...' This stanza invites us to raise our conscious awareness by getting real by living from and as our Real Self which also lives eternally in God's World of unconditional Love. The 'No secrets' is a solution to the highs and lows of our so-often attachment to the ego's drama (which disappears when we let go of our ego's Make-believe false world by remembering to choose God by saying a simple prayer of asking for God's help). [88]
Repeat S-1 through -5 above	Thereby, and then, our 'Heartaches can turn into joy.'

Prayer is essentially unheard of in Rock lyrics, and it is rare even in Pop (here Our prayer will be heard, Make it soon). It is also in Mike's 'Lost in a Lost World' "Come on my friend / We've got to bend / On our knees and say a prayer." Yet the Moodies are so real and creative enough to honor its power here. Imagine the Stones, The Who or <u>you name them</u> even *approaching* that degree of spiritual integrity.

These two stanzas are to us among their most compelling and memorable in all of their work:

> So fly little bird / Up into the clear blue sky
> And carry the word / Love's the only reason why, why...
>
> Open all the shutters on your windows
> Unlock all the locks upon your doors
> Brush away the cobwebs from your daydreams
> No secrets come between us anymore

These powerful words sung and backed so clearly and magnificently are an anthem to our path to perhaps the healthiest relationships we can experience with self, others and God.

The recent Christian-related holy book *A Course in Miracles* describes how we are living in a "dream within a dream." In my book *Choosing God,* I (CW) summarize what *the Course* says about that, and we believe that the Moodies here do that psycho-spiritual observation clear justice.

This song is but one among their many spiritually oriented works. Most of their others came throughout the rest of their core 7. A few came after them in their final eight albums, which we have addressed in the previous chapter and elsewhere in this book.

20 TIMELESS TROUBADOURS

A *Troubadour* is a composer and performer of lyric poetry, a strolling minstrel, poet and singer. The 13th century Italian poet Dante Alighieri defined the troubadour's lyric as rhetorical (i.e., figurative, not literal), musical and poetical fiction (in his literary work *De vulgari eloquentia*). But the Moodies have not limited their work to fiction. Theirs is usually applied to *real life*, which they do so well and which we describe throughout in this book.

Troubadours started about 1100 AD (CE, or the "Common Era" since Jesus). After the "classical" period around the turn of the 13th century, their art declined in the 14th century and eventually died out around the time of the Black Death (1348). [35] It remained underground until several centuries later when it resurfaced in the 19th century as the recently modern musical folk movement. [35]

While the early troubadours recited and sung about courtly love and chilvary, the Moodies have addressed real and often even mature love. Of all the 1960s and early 70s bands, they took real love into an understandable truth and beyond. Listeners and fans who knew identified with their message and continue to enjoy their music.

In Justin's most recent of five solo efforts, he wrote this classic entitled 'Troubadour,' now available on his CD album *A View from the Hill* and also made a great acoustic guitar and voice only solo of it on a You Tube. We describe our summary understanding of its meaning in Table 20.1 below. In a telling review on that album, a fan said, "...Justin Hayward is the greatest living rock love ballad writer. ...Hayward has long been the most under-rated of all the great rockers. What Mick Jagger is to on-stage strut, Justin Hayward is to your heart of heart and soul of your soul." [49]

The early troubadours wandered, performed and thereby "toured," which the Moodies have mastered. In a 1990 radio interview with disc jockey Ed Sciaky in Philadelphia, Justin said, "The Moody Blues has always been a touring band. We've always known that the best way to put our music in front of the people is to tour and so that's what we do. A lot of people want to hear it." [70]

Table 20.1. Making Meaning of Troubadour
by Justin Hayward from his album *A View from the Hill* 1996

Lyrics	Our Suggested Meaning
Troubadour I was only a little boy, when I heard the call Like a voice in the wilderness, that calls to us all	Even though this song does not include the other Moodies, we list it here because it fits this book about them as Timeless Troubadours.
So I took to the gypsy life, in the city of love And I walked with the troubadours And flew with the doves In the city of love	We believe that Justin's words here represent classical and authentic lyrical, vocal and musical creativity at its best. It is primo 'troubadourian.' It happens to be so titled, and written and

In the garden of paradise, I heard a voice sing
I can still feel the thrill of it, the chills it would bring / Far away in the western sky,
over the sea
There's a land that we dream about, peaceful and free
Waiting for me

Hold my hand, let me take you there
Let's go walking in the morning / As time goes by, love will wash us clean / Let love bring to us our freedom

And we will sing of the heroes / And fly on the breeze / Love with the lovers of the world
Oh oh oh...we'll be free

In the dark of the mystic night, music is born / In the hands of the troubadour, the piper of dawn / And it's heard of a foreign shore, over the sea / In the land that we dream about, peaceful and free / Waiting for me
Repeat chorus x 2

sung by perhaps the modern master of the folk, romantic and spiritual genre from the 60s to today.

He refers to love and to a resulting land of freedom and peace four times each. Through his quality and loving values and creativity he has made his life into what he describes throughout these lyrics. As a troubadour he here describes and models his own spiritual path for us to consider.

Throughout their words and music the Moodies tell us in various ways how love is the answer, and here Justin reminds us of that yet again.

He shows us how our creativity so often comes from our unconscious mind In the dark of the mystic night, music is born - as we describe in Chapters 1 and 4 above.

And how he and the Moodies as timeless troubadours have crossed the land and sea as the piper of dawn
by touring with their message of love.

He repeats how being free and freedom can bring about his and our own creativity.

125

For we listeners who know enough about Justin and the Moodies, this song appears to be clearly autobiographical. For those who may not know that, we see the first stanza as essentially the start of his story, and the rest then flowed as his long and creative career unfolded. All 5 Troubadours:

Justin, Graeme and John

Ray   Mike

21 THEIR MESSAGE

While the Moodies' message is many-fold, we believe that it is mostly about relationships and values. Throughout this book we have described how we see that through their music they have helped many to most of us explore our relationships with our self, others and God. Through their words and music they have helped us explore the Divine Mystery (see Glossary and Index). While we have already addressed it from various angles throughout this book, in this last chapter we will look at some more examples of how they deliver their powerful message.

The next three paragraphs below are how I (CW) began the final chapter in my recent book which was on *Core Issues in Relationships, Recovery and Living*. [90] That chapter was on the core issue of *Difficulty Giving and Receiving Love*, and I started it followed by this quote from John's special song.

"Love is paradoxically both the most difficult and—ultimately after a lot of commitment and attention in a relationship—the easiest, but only after we have done the hard work through most of our other core issues. John wrote:

Isn't love strange,
A word we arrange,
With no thought or care,
Maker of despair...

127

Love is usually the most psychologically and spiritually invigorating of our feelings. Yet, most of us have been hurt over love by disappointment, rejection and betrayal. As a result we often become reluctant to risk expressing our love to anyone. And we may not trust others when they express their love to us. So how can we approach giving and receiving love? What do we know about love?"

It is clear to us, and possibly others, perhaps including you, that achieving healthy relationships is often difficult. But when we are real with safe others with whom we may commit and work through our conflicts and issues, we can make them work and even enjoy them. Our experience is that listening to the Moodies and their message—while we do or don't do our recovery work—can assist us in this process. We believe that the above dynamics and more are why so many people have remained their fans for so long.

We outline our understanding of their main messages in the left-hand column of Table 21.1 on the next page. Each involves our relationship with our self, others and God. The content and way the Moodies share these with us is also related to positive and constructive personal and ideal cultural *values* which ultimately enrich our lives. A value is what we find important in our three above relationships. [82] At its most rewarding quality, values are not based on money, material goods or property. In 'One More Time to Live' the Moodies wrote and sang, "I have riches more than these... ."

Table 21.1. The Main Messages of The Moody Blues

Message	Example Songs and Comments
Love	*Nights in White Satin* *My Song* *Say It With Love* *Haunted* *The Land of Make-Believe*
Healthy Relationships	*Have You Heard?* Each involves our *You and Me* relationship with our *The Voice* self, others and God
Expanded Consciousness & Optimism	*Eyes of a Child* *Eternity Road* *Candle of Life* *Out and In One More Time to Live*
Celebration of Our Life Here & Now	*Lovely to See You* *English Sunset* *A Simple Game*

If you have any more of their messages to describe, please consider leaving any on our website for feedback and comments on this book at **MoodiesBook.Wordpress.com**

From our long listening to their words and music and ongoing study of their careers, we have seen how all five of them respect, live and work by these messages and values. Without these they would likely not have been able to start, continue and maintain their creative and successful careers. And their countless loyal fans and their many other spontaneous concert-goers would not have continued to support their ongoing tours across the USA, Canada, New Zealand, Australia, South Africa and the UK as they have to this day.

These 16 songs above that we selected are but examples of those that expressed what we see as their message. We will focus on three of them in this chapter. As examples of their messages, we start below with Justin's 'Say It with Love.' Check it out and when you have time listen on your system.

Table 7.1. Making Meaning of Say It with Love
by Justin Hayward from *Keys of the Kingdom* 1991

Lyrics	Our Suggested Meaning
Say It with Love I've been thinking The way people do 'Bout the things that matter / To me and you / I've decided / To do what I can / And to find the kind of man / I really am I can see the world from here / And it sometimes makes me / Want to disappear / Back to nature / That's where we belong / And with just one truth I've found You can't go wrong Wherever you go Whatever you do Whatever you say / Say, say, say / Say it with love.	This song has no core 7 mystical flavor, but it may be hard to find a more basic spiritual practice sung and played so well as this one. A delightful upbeat little story-in-song about expressing love wherever we go when we are with our relationships in our world. This may be another Moodies' anthem for all we know. It's such a simple and even 'mantric' tune to remember to make our life go well Wherever you go Whatever you do Whatever you say / Say, say, say / Say it with love.
I remember / A long time ago / When I heard those guitars / That I worship so I was captured / I wanted to stay / And to hear that kind of music / Everyday Heard the songs Around the world Saw the smiling faces On the boys and girls I was destined / To play come what may / And there's just one thing I knew I had to say / Wherever you go Whatever you do	The triple "Say" adds a nice melodic harmony that underlines this, perhaps, the Moodies' main message. So many references through their poems-in-song, here again to the personal power of being real ...to find the kind of man I really am i.e., by being my Real Self. Or expressed another way by so many of us a million voices shouting / Let me out, let me out And then, back to nature, of which

130

| Whatever you say
Say, say, say
Say it with love.

Underneath / A sea of doubt / There's a million voices shouting / Let me out, let me out /When we go / We never return 'Cos there's just one lesson / That we got to learn / Wherever you go Whatever you do Whatever you say Say, say, say Say it with love x 5 | we are already and always a part
Back to nature / That's where we belong / And with just one truth I've found
You can't go wrong … Say it with love.

We sense a good autobiographical touch and nicely reminiscent of his 'Troubadour'—
When I heard those guitars / That I worship so I was captured / I wanted to stay / And to hear that kind of music / Everyday / Heard the songs Around the world
Saw the smiling faces / On the boys and girls I was destined / To play come what may |

Too simple? A problem (and some say it is our *only* problem) is that we are too often attached to our *false self*, also known as our *ego*. The modern and, some say Christian-oriented holy book *A Course in Miracles* has the most sophisticated description of the ego— and how to get out of its inherent pain —that we have found in our long and mostly enjoyable lives.

The Course suggests that Love is the solution. It describes that the ego—as a so-called 'player' (in our life's unfolding play)—is actually neither a player nor a person. Rather, the ego is a temporary and illusory kind of assistant or entity that we made, and which God did not make. Why would we make the ego? *The Course* doesn't give a clear answer. Our personal guess is that we made the ego to help us sort and navigate as we journey on this divinely mysterious adventure of our life on this planet. See Table 10.3 at the end of Chapter 10 for more on the ego.

Next is Mike's 'My Song.' These may be among his most telling and important words, among his many other great ones. See what you think, as you peruse them and how we understand their meaning.

Table 7.1. Making Meaning of My Song

by Mike Pinder   1971 last track on *EGBDF*

Lyrics	Our Suggested Meaning
My Song I'm going to sing my song / And sing it all day long / A song that never ends / How can I tell you / All the things inside my head	Although a bit long in its preamble here, it is nonetheless appropriate for preparing us for his and the Moodies', again, message of Love. As most fans know, Love is a basic theme throughout their music.
2 The change in these past years / Has made me see our world In many different ways / How can I tell you? / Love can change our destiny 3 Love can change the world / Love can change your life / Do what makes you happy / Do what you know is right! And love with all your might Before it's too late	We understand *'Right'* here (in S-3) as being about integrity and honesty, living from and as our Real Self, while not hurting others. *Happy* is not about constant pleasure, and it is only temporary. In the long run it is more about attaining inner peace, with fun occurring as often as it happens and with occasional joy. Something inside of me is burning reminds us of Mike's keen and creative introspection throughout his storied career in music. This song reflects how important our inner life of our Real Self is for us in an ongoing way. Mike also

4 Where did I find all these words? Something inside of me is burning There's life in other worlds Maybe they'll come to earth / Helping man to find a way	models the personal power of being real and vulnerable here— which the other band members have also modeled in their lyrics. Where did I find all these words? His '*words*' here strengthen the meaning of his writings now and in others' on healthy relationships.
5 One day I hope we'll be / in perfect harmony A planet with one mind / Then I could tell you / All the things inside my head Repeat S-1 I'm going to sing my song / A song that never ends...	As do many of their songs, he reminds us of our higher levels of awareness and consciousness. These are universal insights of many of us who have experienced spiritual awakenings (sometimes called spiritually transformative experiences, as we describe in Chapter 8).

Finally, one of their most fun songs is Justin's and the Moodies' lively, but again powerful, 'Lovely to See You.'

To see them perform this classic Moodies' message song, get a copy of their 2005 concert in Los Angeles' Greek Theater, with 18 other songs in high quality video and sound. Or search Youtube.

We have covered 'The Land of Make-Believe' in Chapter 19 above and many of their other great poems-in-music in Table 21.1 elsewhere throughout this book.

Table 7.1. Making Meaning of Lovely to See You
by Justin Hayward 1969 from *OtToaD*

Lyrics	Our Suggested Meaning
Lovely To See You Wonderful day for passing my way Knock on my door, even the score With your eyes Lovely to see you again, my friend Walk along with me to the next bend Dark cloud of fear is blowing away Now that you're here, you're going to stay 'Cause it's... Repeat S-2 Tell us what you've seen In faraway forgotten lands Where empires have turned back to sand Repeat S-1 & 2 x2	A delightful celebration of our life in the here and now when we encounter another or others and continue being with them in any kind of positive relationship. Expresses the ideal and upside of healthy and fulfilling relationships anywhere along the spectrum from casual acquaintances to long term committed ones. The dark cloud of my or our fear, perhaps in a strained relationship time wherein you left me, is now gone since you are back with me and us to stay. Tell us what you've seen In faraway forgotten lands ... In another song-within-a-song, our poet invites us to share, in perhaps another troubadourian fashion, about our life's travels and many experiences. Of course, mystical references to ancient lands 'Where empires have turned back to sand' are common among the Moodies' masterpieces.

134

Exactly what have they done to make their message so easy to hear? We can find no better summary of their vast work than Childs and March's chapters from their fine recent book on pop music stars: "The Moody Blues have created a majestic musical legacy, characterized by thoughtful, sophisticated lyrics, impeccably crafted arrangements, shimmering production, and brilliant musicianship." [9]

No question.

Their music enfolded their powerful message.

NB: For anyone interested in seeing how we have made meaning for seven more selected Moodies' songs that we did not cover in the above chapters, we include them below at the end of the Appendix in the 'Orchestra Seating' Section, subtitled as
→ *More Songs* for Making Meaning.

APPENDIX
TIME LINE FOR THE MOODY BLUES

Band 1 history 1955-1966

1955 American rhythm and blues and "skiffle" music begins to inspire and influence many young British musicians, including especially those in the Erdington/Birmingham, England area. (*See tree figures* six pages *below* showing various band members and their connections with other groups.)

1958 Ray Thomas forms "Saints and Sinners" band and later "El Riot and the Rebels" with Mike Pinder in Birmingham. 14 Y.O. John Lodge participates some. Shortly later, John leaves the band and starts college

1963 Mike Pinder briefly joins the British Army. Then he returns later with Ray Thomas, Graeme Edge, Denny Laine and Clint Warwick to form "The M and B 5" band on 4 May 1964 (Mitchells and Butlers Brewery pubs where they had hoped to perform.) To finish college, John temporarily declines joining them.

1964 They eventually use the name The Moody Blues. Base some of their music on American R&B and Bessie Banks gospel songs, which inspires their Merseybeat/R&B hit "Go Now." They meet the Beatles who were rising in popularity and open for them at some concerts. Develop first Decca album *The Magnificent Moodies,* released in 1965; a management was reported to take much of their profits.

Meanwhile Justin Hayward works with Marty Wilde for two years in "The Wilde Three" and "All Things Bright" bands.

1966 In June Clint Warwick leaves band. Then in October Denny Laine leaves. John Lodge re-joins. Financial distress continues. Their creativity remains about the same. They look for a lead guitar and vocalist.

Band 2 history 1966 to present

1966 In about December Mike, Ray and band hire Justin. Band tries to make a success by continuing R&B and fails. Eventually, all 5 members agree to change. Discard old suits, music and style. "Band 1" ends.

1967 March: Begin writing and performing own music in a stage show, and become popular in France. They add distinctive words and uplifting melody, esp. when Mike finds a Mellotron for £80. "Band 2" thus begins. Creativity increases among all 5 members.

September: Decca executive producer Hugh Mendl asks them to do a rock version of Dvorak's NW Symphony for Decca's new stereo format. MBs ask to do their stage show music. Peter Knight arranges symphonic track with sound engineer Derek Varnals who record separately from MBs stage show, using the 'London Festival Orchestra' to provide full orchestral backing between their songs on the album, with rock instrumentation centered on Pinder's Mellotron. Combine the two as *Days of Future Past* (DoFP) representing a musical day in the life of an ordinary person, released 11 November. Decca's Tony Clarke produces this and all later albums for the next 11 years.

1968 DoFP sells well. In next album, *In Search of the Lost Chord* (ISotLC) MBs drop symphony orchestra and experiment with various instruments to make new sounds. Released 26 July. Concerts and tours increase, including in USA with success.

1969 Write and compose *two* more core 7 big seller albums *in one year*:
• *On the Threshold of a Dream* (OtToaD) 25 April,

• *To Our Children's Children's Children* (TOCCC) 21 *November,* 7 months later (some say their best ever).

1970 Then, and only 5 months later, *A Question of Balance* (AQoB) on 25 April. *Summary*: 3 high quality and big selling albums *in 12 months*, a remarkable creative achievement.

1971 *Every Good Boy Deserves Favor* (EGBDF) 23 July

1972 *Seventh Sojourn* (SS) 17 November

1974 (April) to **1977** Members take a hiatus for about 3 years, writing and performing mostly independently.

1977 30 April   *Caught Live +5* (former songs from 1960s)

1978 9 June   *Octave* (also a basic term in all music)

Members reunite temporarily, go back on tour. Mike Pinder leaves to be with his family.

Former *Yes* keyboardist Patrick Moraz takes his place (wrote no Moodies' songs) until 1991.

1981 15 May   *Long Distance Voyager*

1983 23 August   *The Present*

1986 30 May *Other Side of Life*

Mid 1980s *MTV exposure* helped by Tony Visconti, with an increase in their fan base of younger listeners and music sales.

1987 *Prelude* –an album from Band 2 pre-*DoFP* "transitional" period; 12 less known but some good to excellent tracks (a modified compilation)

1988 6 June   *Sur La Mer*

1989 30 October   *Legend of a Band*: The Story of the Moody Blues and Selected songs.

17 November *Greatest Hits* (compilation)

1991 25 June   *Keys of the Kingdom*

Keyboardist Patrick Moraz leaves

1993 3 March DVD concert 'A Night at the Red Rocks' Released 2002

1994 27 September   *Time Traveler* (Outstanding 5 CD set of most of their best, with excellent commentary text and many color photos)

1997 28 January *The Best of the Moody Blues*. Selected songs (compilation) Good sleeve notes

1998 20 October   *Anthology* (compilation)

1999 17 August   *Strange Times*

2000 *Best of the Moody Blues: Millennium*.

8 August 'Hall of Fame' concert Live at Royal Albert Hall in London DVD, released 2002

2001 24 April Instrumental music *Journey into Amazing Caves* (soundtrack, with various artists. Does not sound like classic Moodies.)

2002 Ray Thomas leaves band after fall concert tour; Flautist and vocalist Norda Mullen replaces him. She continues to the present with success.

2003 14 January *Say it with Love* CD (compilation)

2003 3 March A Night at the Red Rocks concert (deluxe DVD) Released 2008

28 October *December* album

2005 1 March *Gold* (compilation)

25 September *Chronicles* (boxed set of first 3 albums)

15 November Concert 'Live at the Greek,' in Los Angeles, released on DVD 2008

2006 29 August *Introduction to the Moody Blues* CD (compilation)

2007 17 April *Live at the BBC* 1967-1970 CD released (compilation)

2008 28 April *Play list Plus* 3 CD set of classic songs (compilation)

25 August Live at the Isle of Wight DVD Documentary of concert released. In late August 1970, shortly after the release of the 5th of their core 7 album AQoB, they took to the stage of the 'Isle of Wight Festival' in front of an audience estimated at over half a million. This well-filmed with good sound and well edited DVD makes their now classic and outstanding performance available for the first time.

2013 Have sold over 70 million albums worldwide, awarded 14 platinum and gold discs, remain active creating and touring with one from 1964's Band 1 (Graeme) and two more from the 1966/7 Band 2 (Justin and John). Sales continue at 500 K albums/year. Since they began, countless fans, and with concert tours, have followed and still follow them.

It's Not Easy to become a Star The 'Ten-Year Rule' continues (*see* Table G 2 below).
Fun Trivia and a 'Family Tree,' from 1958

The **Saints and Sinners** were formed by Mike Brassington (vocals, guitar) in March 1958, with: Brian "Miff" Smith, Guitar, Dave Jones, Percussion, Ricky Wade, Washboard, drums, 16-year-old **Ray Thomas**, 'Tea-chest,' double bass). Ray, a tool maker trainee from age 15, heard that the band was looking for a bass player and had found Mike Brassington. A 'skiffle' group, inspired by Lonnie Donegan, they played gigs in and around Erdington, Birmingham. They became a vocal and rhythm band until June 1959 when they departed and joined other groups or formed a new band.

Then came **El Riot** and the **Rebels** (*see next page*) where 15-year-old **John Lodge** and 18-year-old **Mike Pinder** did a short stint before Mike joined the UK military. While serving he also played keyboards and sang, entertaining his mates while stationed in Germany—*and* where he soon encountered the Hamburg rock scene. John had also left for college.

Once back in Birmingham Mike and Ray formed the **Krew Kats**, specifically to take advantage of playing in Germany. They played at the Top Ten Club in Hamburg (famous for featuring the Beatles), but the group disbanded after a couple of months, leaving Ray and Mike stranded in Hamburg just before Christmas with no money or transportation back to Birmingham. They started walking. It was freezing and 417 miles away. It took them over a week, with little sleep and only a few snacks to eat. They limped into Oostende, Belgium and the British Consulate which reluctantly loaned them just enough money to get safely back to Birmingham.

Eventually they joined with **Graeme Edge** (*see next page*), Denny Laine and Clint Warwick to form what they soon called The M & B 5, then The Moody Blues Five, and later simply The Moody Blues (Band 1). Around this time, **Mike Pinder** was also employed by Streetly Electronics that made the Mellotron.

On the next two pages we show the Moodies' **"Family Tree"** that adds another dimension to their Timeline and history we have detailed throughout this book. Note that it *does not include* the Saints and Sinners and the Krew Kats, which we describe above. Several of these other musicians, such as Roy Wood and Bev Bevan later went on to other bands as ELO, etc.

GERRY LEVINE and The AVENGERS
Early 1963 until April 1964

GERRY LEVINE	ROY WOOD	MIKE HOPKINS	JIM ONSLOW	GRAEME EDGE
vocals	guitar	guitar	bass/vocals	drums

EL RIOT and The REBELS
1959 until Spring 1963

RAY THOMAS	Mike PINDER	JOHN LODGE	MICKEY HERD	BRIAN BETTERIDGE	BOBBY SHURE
voc/harp	keyboards	bass	rhythm	lead	drums

WILDE THREE
July 1964 until Sept 1965

JUSTIN HAYWARD	MARTY WILDE	JOYCE WILDE
guitar/vocals	guitar/vocals	vocals

DENNY LAINE and The DIPLOMATS
Sept 1962 until April 1964

BEV BEVAN	PHIL ACKRILL	STEVE HORTON	DENNY LAINE
drums	guitar/vocals	bass	guitar/vocals

MOODY BLUES #1
May 1964 until October 1966

CLINT WARWICK	DENNY LAINE	MIKE PINDER	RAY THOMAS	GRAEME EDGE
bass	guitar/vocals	keybd	vocals/harp	drums

REFUGEE
August 1973 until August 1964

LEE JACKSON	PATRICK MORAZ	BRIAN DAVISON
bass/vocals	keyboards	drums

142

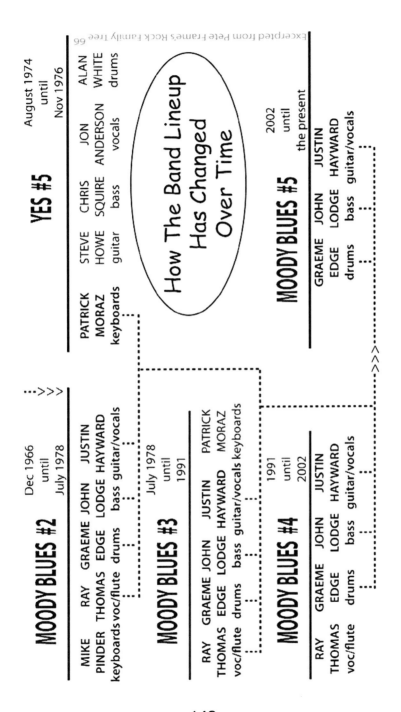

How The Band Lineup Has Changed Over Time

YES #5

August 1974 until Nov 1976

PATRICK MORAZ keyboards · STEVE HOWE guitar · CHRIS SQUIRE bass · JON ANDERSON vocals · ALAN WHITE drums

MOODY BLUES #2

Dec 1966 until July 1978

MIKE PINDER keyboards · RAY THOMAS voc/flute · GRAEME EDGE drums · JOHN LODGE bass · JUSTIN HAYWARD guitar/vocals

MOODY BLUES #3

July 1978 until 1991

RAY THOMAS voc/flute · GRAEME EDGE drums · JOHN LODGE bass · JUSTIN HAYWARD guitar/vocals · PATRICK MORAZ keyboards

MOODY BLUES #4

1991 until 2002

RAY THOMAS voc/flute · GRAEME EDGE drums · JOHN LODGE bass · JUSTIN HAYWARD guitar/vocals

MOODY BLUES #5

2002 until the present

GRAEME EDGE drums · JOHN LODGE bass · JUSTIN HAYWARD guitar/vocals

Glossary

Table G.1 Definitions of Music Terms

Melody Said to be the **single most important** aspect of music. [25] A linear succession of tones in a combination of pitch and rhythm. May be in foreground and/or background. (aka Tune or Line) Also called the horizontal or linear aspect, with *harmony* as the vertical aspect (below).

In most of their songs the **Moodies'** melodies are engaging, enlivening and fun to hear.

Timbre or **Sound** The actual physical sound or tone color made by one or more instruments,* including our *voice.* [5, 25, 96] This is one of the **Moodies'** characteristics that have been outstanding since Band 2 started in 1967 with *DoFP*.

Pitch A *discrete* sound part, characterized by a fundamental sound *frequency* across the musical scale, [25] e.g., in : "do re mi fa so la ti do..." The notes of the scale are ordered in pitch or pitch class. Even today, the **MBs** delivery of pitch and harmony remains remarkable.

Rhythm/Beat/Tempo The shortest division among sounds to which we can execute on an instrument, dance or move. [25] We see the **Moodies'** *beat* being at the top among the best of popular and rock musicians. *Tempo* is the *speed* of the beat. *Meter* is how the beats are *grouped in time* (below).

Meter How beats are grouped in a section of music. The *pattern* of lines and accents in the verse of a poem, song, ballad or hymn. Music has inherited this useful term from the rhythmic element of poetry.

Lyric pertains to the lyre, adopted for singing with the Greek classical instrument. As we describe throughout this book, the **MB**s were master lyricists.

Motif or **Motive** A short musical idea, recurring figure, musical fragment or succession of notes that has some special importance in or is characteristic of a composition: "The motive is the smallest structural unit possessing thematic identity." [25]

Harmony Two or more pitches happening at the same time, aka the vertical dimension of musical space. The simultaneous relationship of and among tones and pitches. Harmony is indivisible from melody [25] [which is horizontal/linear].

Chord Three or more pitches expressed at the same time; a chord is one of the most fundamental parts of harmony. Of course, their 2nd, *ISoLC,* used it in the title.

Texture is the *way* the melodic, rhythmic, and harmonic sounds are *combined*. The number and relationship of and among different melodies present in a section. The range or width between lowest and highest pitches according to the number of voices or parts and the relationship between these voices. A more sophisticated **Moodies'** strength. [25, 75]

Secondary melody Shares the basic melody with the foreground or thematic melody briefly. Essential and crucial to enrich a piece. Another **Moodies'** strength. [25]

Song-within-a-song A musical characteristic the **Moodies** have perfected. E.g., heard in Question, Never Comes the Day, Tuesday Afternoon, Floating, The Actor, English Sunset, and more.

Octave The essential building block of pitch systems. A technical term difficult to understand: It is the interval between one pitch and another with half or double its frequency. It may be derived from the harmonic series as the interval between the first and second harmonics. [25] Of course, it was the **Moodies'** eighth album title.

Tone A *steady,* periodic sound characterized by its duration, pitch, intensity (or loudness), and timbre (or quality). The *notes* used in music can be more complex than musical tones. [25]

Poetry The art of expressing thoughts, feelings, ideas, observations, experiences and facts in verse. We and others believe that the **MBs** poetic lyrics are *unsurpassed* in classic and progressive rock.

Story Songs as short stories set to poetry and music. Vary in seriousness.

Message Love others, God and self (healthy self caring). See Chapter 21 for full message.

Mind expanding Hearing nearly all of the **Moodies'** music expands our mind, heart and spirit.

OVERALL

The **Moodies** have blended essentially all of the above music's characteristics into an ideal and winning combination as a highly successful band that has maintained a vast and loyal fan base for nearly five decades. To our knowledge, no other band has done so.

*Instruments may be: stringed, wind, brass, percussion, keyboards; of course electronic instruments may imitate these in varying degrees of accuracy and quality. But they cannot compete with the most basic and still most sophisticated instrument: our voice. The **Moodies** again excel in vocal excellence to this day.

Table G.2 Definitions of Key Psycho-Spiritual Terms Related to Moodies' Music and Message

Consciousness Awareness of both our outer life and especially inner life. It includes how awake we are to these aspects, our ability to experience and feel, having a sense of real selfhood, and it involves our own "executive" control system of our mind. Part of it includes anything that we are aware of at any given moment, making *conscious experience* at once the most familiar and most mysterious aspect of our lives. It is a key part of the Divine Mystery (see below). [11, 24, 27, 39, 74, 83]

Altered State of Consciousness/Awareness (ASC) Can be *self-induced* by using sensory deprivation, an isolation tank, sleep deprivation; in lucid dreaming, hypnosis, meditation, prayer, or various disciplines (e.g., Mantra Meditation, Yoga, out-of-body experience or astral projection.) ASCs can also be attained through the ingestion of psychoactive drugs such as alcohol and opiates, but more commonly with the traditional psychedelics (mind expanding and soul nourishing) of indigenous cultures, plants such as cannabis, psilocybin mushrooms, Peyote, and Ayahuasca, and other psychedelics as LSD-25. [36, 74, 86]

ASCs can occur *accidentally* through, e.g., fever, infections such as meningitis, sleep deprivation, fasting, oxygen deprivation, nitrogen narcosis (deep diving), during childbirth, psychosis, temporal lobe epilepsy or a traumatic accident. During an ASC, brain waves occupy different categories of frequencies (i.e. Epsilon, Delta, Theta, Alpha, Beta, and Gamma). These waves can be measured using an EEG.

Spirituality Search for meaning, connection to nature, humanity, unity, and the transcendent. (Emmons)

A vast experience that ultimately involves a direct connection to a Higher Power (C Whitfield)

Mystical Experience A deviation from our ordinary conscious awareness that transcends ordinary experience and manifests as a direct, intimate, and intuitive encounter with a reality of a higher order of magnitude. [36, 41, 86]

Divine Mystery "I believe there is something of the divine mystery in everything that exists. We can see it sparkle in a sunflower or a poppy. We sense more of the unfathomable mystery in a butterfly that flutters from a twig—or in a goldfish swimming in a bowl. But we are closest to God in our own soul. Only there can we become one with the greatest mystery of life. In truth, at very rare moments we can experience that we ourselves *are* that divine mystery." Jostein Gaarder, from *Sophie's World.* In their words and music the **Moodies** are repeatedly exploring and expressing the Mystery.

Real Self/Child Within/Eyes of a Child This is our True Self, our true identity, the only part of us that can connect with and authentically relate to self, others and God. [87, 90, 91]

false self/ego This is who we so often pretend to be when we feel unsafe or we fear others judging or hurting us. *A Course in Miracles* says we can know that we are in our *ego* when we are *not at peace.*

Creativity Mental and social process involving the discovery of new ideas, concepts, or products—or new associations of the creative mind between existing ideas or concepts. [27,94]

'Big C' Creativity is another term we use for creative performances or products of a grand scale which are socially judged to merit recognition and approval. [R&R Hall of Fame promoters appear to have a limited definition and awareness of real creativity and music art. The **MB**s have wisely remained detached from the drama.]

'Little c' creativity includes creative expressions, behaviors, performances and products that we develop to address everyday problems or tasks and do not typically receive social recognition. We can use these to our good in our relationships.

Freedom is the innate right to determine our personal action without restraint. It is a necessity for being creative. The **Moodies** had enough freedom early to create their music. But later it has become more difficult for all musicians. Answering the question, "Today, could there be a group like the Moody Blues?" **Ray** Thomas said, "No. There are not the gigs that we did, playing in pubs, local churches. Today you make a record, do a little disc or two, and you're finished. *We* worked with musicians, 'men of music.' Today you work with lawyers. I was lucky, probably. But the more you work hard, the more fortune gives you a chance."

Peak Experience An experience of revelations or illuminations accompanied with a feeling of euphoria.

Synchronicity is basically meaningful coincidence. It includes the simultaneous or near simultaneous happening of coincidental events which have no [common] cause. The odd events, because of their occurrence so close in time, are instilled with meaning by those who recognize them. [58] Jung called it the simultaneous occurrence of two, or more, meaningful events that are not causally connected. C&BW: Synchronicity is guided by the Divine. Guided/destined to bring truth, and thus healing; a high spiritual energy.

Serendipity means discovery by accident and sagacity, of things not sought for. When a person accidentally discovers something that they were not originally seeking (Walpole). Serendipity is related to luck. [May help explain a few but not all reasons why **MB**s wrote such great poetry.]

Archetype Originally meant "first-moulded," later as a universally understood symbol, term, statement, or pattern of behavior, a prototype upon which others are copied, patterned, or emulated. Archetypes are often used in myths and storytelling across different cultures. [3] [Almost never naming God directly, the **MB**s make several archetypal allusions or associations, such as indirect references to a Higher Power, the Universe, love, freedom, our Real Self indirectly as Eyes of a Child, the wizard-as-advisor archetype of Merlin (see cover art) and others].

Ten-year Rule The empirical generalization in the field of creativity that, on average, it requires about a decade of intense study and practice to acquire world-class expertise in most domains of achievement. Data also suggest that ten years of work, or ten thousand hours (about 3.8 hours a day for ten years), need to be invested into a domain for expertise to develop. [**MB**s took about 10 years from the mid-to-late 1950s to 1967 to begin to show their creative musical expertise.]

Near-death Experience Refers to a broad range of personal experiences associated with impending death, encompassing multiple possible sensations including detachment from the body, feelings of levitation, total serenity, security, or warmth, the experience of absolute dissolution, and the presence of a loving light. [86]

Spiritually Transformative Experience (STE) An experience that causes people to perceive themselves and the world profoundly differently: by expanding their identity, augmenting their sensitivities, and thereby altering their values, priorities and appreciation of the purpose of life. STEs may be triggered by surviving clinical death, or by otherwise experiencing an enlarged reality. Other triggers for this experience are: Childbirth, experiencing the death of a loved one and other great losses, working a Twelve Step program, meditation, deep prayer, in the presence of a great spiritual teacher, what is called "A Big Dream," or taking psychedelic drugs. The after effects are usually so profound that the experiencer can't ignore them nor do they usually want to. They often have a sense of mission that may take a lifetime to understand and a need to practice all the Higher Needs of Abraham Maslow's hierarchy of needs, especially the desire and need for love as the experiencer believes Love was meant to be. There also can be a time alteration so that linear time less often rules daily experience. Materialism usually decreases and the Golden Rule becomes the ideal. For some there is a great longing to go back to the experience or to change their life so they can live by the new standards.

Stages of Healing and Recovery These parallel the levels of consciousness (see Figure 4.1 in Chapter 4) and cover active acute or chronic illness of any kind at **Stage Zero** to **Stage 1** (where conventional medical treatments may begin to stabilize and sometimes cure it). But Stage 1 treatments cure most chronic illness much *less often* because that is so often due to the effects of repeated childhood and later trauma, as are especially so for symptoms of "*mental illness*," (which are nearly always *trauma based*.) [90, 91]

Stage 2 is where these trauma effects are most effectively addressed, helped and often healed. **Stage 3** involves using spirituality and spiritual practices. [90, 91] The **Moodies'** psycho-spiritually optimistic and uplifting music and message may play a small but useful role.

'Orchestra Seating' Section
→ *More Songs* for Making Meaning

For anyone interested in seeing how we have made meaning for the following seven additional Moodies' songs that we did not cover in the above chapters, we include them below.

The Story in Your Eyes   The title alone is itself a perfect symbol for the rest of the poem.
This meaningful stream-of-consciousness verse expressed vocally and musically is about as good as it gets (Table A.1).

It was the 2ⁿᵈ song on *EGBDF* (their 6ᵗʰ core 7 album). It is preceded by the short 'Procession' part 1 which was the only song that was said to be written by all five members. That one was intended to describe the history of music from the beginning of time, and the only 3 words in the whole piece are "desolation", "creation", and "communication." In its extension 'One More Time to Live' as song 6 later on *EGBDF* it greatly expands that simple introduction (see after 'Story...' in Table A.2).

Table A.1. Making Meaning of The Story in Your Eyes
by Justin Hayward   1971 in *EGBDF*

Lyrics	Our Suggested Meaning
The Story In Your Eyes I've been thinking about our fortune And I've decided that we're really not to blame / For the love that's deep inside us now	Its music to the story in your eyes continues the 'Eyes of a Child' motif that John and the band had introduced in 1969 so clearly in TOCCC two albums before. We see the 'music' here and

Is still the same And the sounds we make together Is the music to the story in your eyes It's been shining down upon me now I realize Listen to the tide slowly turning / Wash all our heartaches away We're part of the fire that is burning And from the ashes we can build another day But I'm frightened for your children That the life that we are living is in vain And the sunshine we've been waiting for / Will turn to rain Repeat S-3 Repeat S-4 When the final line is over / It's certain that the curtain's gonna fall / I can hide inside your sweet, sweet love Forever more	... the sounds we make together **as representing the many *ways* we *communicate* as our Real Self with one another as we live throughout our life's unfolding stories.** What is the 'it' that has been shining down upon me now that I now realize? **Is it the music of communicating our love that the Moodies write and sing about so often?** **Justin and the band go underneath the music in our expressed love and here describe their worries in as rich and figurative a poetic language as we can imagine** ... tide slowly turning / Wash all our heartaches away / We're part of the fire that is burning / And from the ashes we can build another day. **Their fear may reflect the long Vietnam war of the time. Or that nations have continued to fight for millennia? Or deeper, our basic conflict with our attachment to our ego that always wants to be right and in control?** **No matter what, the conflict will end when we maintain our love.**

Table A.2. Making Meaning of One More Time to Live
by John Lodge 1971 in *EGBDF*

Lyrics	Our Suggested Meaning
One More Time to Live Look out of my window / See the world passing by	In 1997 Stu Werbin of *Rolling Stone Magazine* called this "...the most powerful and most intricate

See the look in her eye

One more time to live and I have made it mine / Leave the wise to write for they write worldly rhymes / And he who wants to fight begins the end of time / For I have riches more than these
For I have riches more than these
Desolation / Creation
Evolution / Pollution
Saturation /Population
Annihilation/Revolution
Confusion / Illusion
Conclusion / Starvation
Degradation/Humiliation
Contemplation
Inspiration / Elation
Salvation
Communication
Compassion / ~~Solution

Look out on the hedgerow / As the world rushes by / Hear the birds sing a sigh / One more tree will fall, how strong the growing vine Turn the earth to sand and still commit no crime / How one thought will live provide the others die / For I have riches more than these x 2

Repeated last lines we show on right in brackets

number on the album..." John McFerrin picked it and 'Story...' as his two best songs in this album.

On the same EGBDF album we see this as *another* meaningful stream-of-consciousness poem expressed in sound and also as good as it gets. Said to be an elaboration on the first song 'Procession,' which was originally about summarizing the history of music in these three words.

We see the phrase he who wants to fight begins the end of time as describing the false self/ego's common focus. Then John's great line I have riches more than these (seeing ... the world passing by as material goods and 'power') is appropriately repeated several times throughout.

Some have told us they skipped this section sometime when they started hearing these 21 –ation words. They are perfect terms for some of our human experience over many of our eras, including the '60s (which actually extended from about 1963 through '74). Additions:

[Tell me someone why there's only confusion; revolution; illusion; revolution; evolution]
[Tell me someone] x 2
[Changes in my life] x 4

Repeat the 21 '-ations
Repeat [Tell me someone... above
Repeat S-1

English Sunset The sometimes controversial Russian music critic George Starotsin called it "… ridiculous techno beats that Hayward employs on the lead-in number, 'English Sunset', nearly ruining a nice, pretty pop song in the process." Others and we disagree, seeing it as one of an unexpected *small few* from their final eight albums they made after their core 7 that rank with their best and that we love enough to keep playing. What has been your experience?

Table A.3. Making Meaning of English Sunset
by Justin Hayward in *Strange Times* 1999

Lyrics	Our Suggested Meaning
English Sunset I want to ride the range / Across those skies of black / I want to see for myself And see me coming back And when I've gone the distance I'll be making tracks / For an English sunset We're on a runaway train Rolling down the track / And where it's taking us to Who knows where it's at / But if we hold together We can make it back / For an English sunset We want an	We see list this song as another example of their message in Chapter 21 above as a **Celebration of Our Life Here & Now.** Justin published this in 1999 when he was 53-years-old. As much as he and the band were away from their home country touring, we understand how sentimental it likely was for him and them to develop and perform this celebration, including in 2002 in London's Royal Albert Hall in front of that sell-out crowd from the UK and all over. Its beauty expands because even today by watching it on DVD we can share by enjoying it and some 16 other Moodies songs, including Ray Thomas' last filmed

English sunset I feel the rhythm of the earth In my soul tonight May it never fade away / And I've decided I can live With humility And the sad decay 'Cause that's the English way [England!] We keep the faith alive / In everything we do And at the end of the road / We still keep coming through / And though it's sad and sorry / What else can we do? It's an English sunset An English sunset [More tea, Vicar?] I feel the rhythm of the earth / In my soul tonight May it never fade away / And I've decided they can wait / For the requiem / We take it day by day 'Cause that's the English way I saw the English sunset	concert wherein he and the band perform 'Legend of a Mind,' a perhaps unusual celebration in song as well. As we said in Chapter 8, I feel the rhythm of the earth In my soul tonight May it never fade away is such a deeply spiritual celebratory expression wherein the music moves our souls just as these powerful words are describing. Humility is a personally powerful place to be even as we celebrate. Is 'the sad decay' the English sun setting? Or is it the sadness of aging or experiencing another loss in his or our life? Or for England? We keep the faith alive In everything we do is what the Moodies have been about and doing since 1967. And perhaps we can too. The 'requiem' is the mass music played at a funeral, for which 'they' or the others can wait, because 'we' take it day by day in the here and now as we celebrate.

Watching and Waiting This one spans the entire levels of consciousness and healing (see Chap 4).

Table A.4. Making Meaning of Watching and Waiting
by Justin Hayward & Ray Thomas 1969, to conclude *TOCCC*

Lyrics	Our Suggested Meaning
Watching and Waiting Watching and waiting / For a friend to play with Why have I been alone so long? Mole he is burrowing His way to the sunlight / He knows there's someone there so strong 'Cause here, there's lots of room for doing / The things you've always been denied / Look and gather all you want to / There's no one here to stop you trying Soon you will see me / 'Cause I'll be all around you But where I come from, I can't tell But don't be alarmed / By my fields and my forests They're here for only you to share 'Cause here there's lot of room for doing The things you've always been denied So look and gather all you want to There's no one here to stop you trying	This is to us another great potential 2-level love relationship poem. Wanting one or more healthy relationships is a nearly universal human experience. Mole burrowing is an image or metaphor that pulls us into our powerful unconscious mind where creativity abounds. The sunlight is a path to the strength of experientially knowing God and the Divine within. With this spiritual knowledge we can now open and grow. Who is the 'me' we will see all around us? Is it a prospective lover or intimate one? Could it be our direct connection to God? Or is the 'me' both? Are my fields and forests the dimensions and experiences of our relationships with ourself, others and God? What Again, with this new spiritual knowledge, including our God given freedom - no one here to stop you trying - we can now open our

Watching and waiting For someone to understand me I hope it won't be very long	awareness to self, others and God, and thereby grow. Watching and waiting For someone to understand me

This is one most of us can identify with, as we long for healthy, real, fun and safe relationships. We sometimes play this before our talks on relationships to set the stage on the importance of being real.

A Simple Game Although recorded in 1968 as the 'B' side to their UK hit single 'Ride My See Saw' on Deram, it was never released on any of their core 7 albums. But it was released on side 3 of their late 1974 compilation album *This Is The Moody Blues,* a two LP (later two CDs) while the band was on a sabbatical.

All of those songs were previously released on earlier albums—except this one. It was then issued later in 1987 in *Prelude* (a modified compilation album) and in 2008 as a 'bonus' track on their remastered SACD version of *ISoLC*.

Mike won an Ivor Novello Award for it in 1968, and this song, plus Pinder's other *OtToaD* song 'So Deep Within You' (1969), were both later successfully recorded by The Four Tops. His son Matt Pinder said: "The four tops recorded it with Tony Clarke producing and dad and Justin singing background vocals. Dad says singing background with the tops was a nice experience."

Even the 'mad Russian' George Starotsin liked it: "It starts off quietly and unpretentiously, and then suddenly, wheez! —and it turns into a swooping anthem with angelic backing vocals and a tremendous level of energy and emotion." [73] Try it.

Table A.5. Making Meaning of A Simple Game
by Mike Pinder 1968, bonus track in *ISoLC remaster* 2008

Lyrics	Our Suggested Meaning
A Simple Game As time goes by you will see / That we're going to be free You and me, we'll touch the sky Can you see in your mind's eye / That we are one / We're all the same / And life is just a simple game There, by your side, I will be / When this crazy world is free Free from doubt When it finds out Exactly what we're meant to be / That we are one / We're all the same / And life is just a simple game Thoughts of another day / Flashing through my head / Thinking how life could be / All of the things that our great men have said / Be what we	We tried to keep our above chapters short for simplicity and focus, but this great poem-song would still have fit neatly into *several* of them. These would include at least four Chapters: # 4. 'The Spectrum of Consciousness,' 8. 'Their Music, Spirituality and the Near-Death Experience,' 19. 'Stage Three Healing,' & 21. 'Their Message.' It addresses several of of Mike's and the Moodies' great themes or 'motifs,' such as the crucial life conditions and experiences of 1) individual freedom, 2) unity consciousness (experiencing oneness with others and God), and the power of 3) taking responsibility for our own life and well-being, as they sing Be what we want to be / What we deserve to be / What we are meant to be. They repeat this refrain beautifully: That we are one / We're all the same / And life is just a simple game some three times. He and the band sing the word 'free' *seven* times. Freedom is a necessity for our being creative. The Moodies had enough freedom early to create

| want to be / What we deserve to be / What we are meant to be

Repeat S-1
We're gonna be free / Oohhh, gonna be free
Gonna be free ... | their music. But later it has become more difficult for all musicians. And, as a side bar, more difficult for too many of us as any government or authority gets so big that they stifle our natural creativity.
We are already and always naturally creative and spiritual. He finishes with three powerful suggestions: Be what we want to be / What we deserve to be / What we are meant to be. One of Mike's best songs. |

The Actor is yet another romantic lyric-poem from Justin, who was about 21 when he wrote it. Critic fan John McFerrin called it "awesome" (we agree, but a trite overused word most of the time). A fan said, "...Once known as the defining MB 'acid' album, *ISotLC* will become known as the album that contained 'The Actor' ... a real gem for the ages." What happens for you when you listen to it?

Table A.6. Making Meaning of The Actor
by Justin Hayward 1968, from *ISoLC*

Lyrics	Our Suggested Meaning
The Actor The curtain rises on the scene / With someone chanting to be free / The play unfolds before my eyes / There stands the actor who is me The sleeping hours takes us far	This is said to be one of Justin's signature love ballads. On the surface it tells the story of a young woman who falls in love with an actor. However, this love is unrequited, since she only sees the actor once when "The Curtain rises." Who or what is the Actor? Beneath the surface we may consider that the main character or player is "the actor," who of course is a fake—

Through traffic,
telephones & fear
Put out your
problems with the
cat / Escape until a
bell you hear

Our reasons are
the same / But
there's no one we
can blame / For
there's nowhere
we need go / And
the only truth we
know
Comes so easily

The sound I have
heard in your hello
Oh, darlin', you're
almost part of me
Oh, darlin', you're
all I'll ever see

It's such a rainy
afternoon / No
point in going
anywhere / The
sounds just drift
across my room
I wish this feeling
I could share

It's such a rainy
afternoon / She sits
and gazes from her
window / Her mind
tries to recall his
face / The feeling
deep inside her
grows /

Repeat S-3

The sound I have

which most all actors are. In Hollywood, professional actors are paid and told to pretend they are someone else. The biggest fake is our ego, below.

The Moodies are not actors. They were young in their 20s and now are in their late 60s and early 70s doing what they love, which is real. They still love singing and projecting their loving words and music onto their fans who still pay them well to remind us of the spiritual gifts God has given us but which we may have forgotten about when we are in our ego's default mode. Then their fans project *their* love back to them in a win-win experience.

But in real life the ego or false self doesn't usually work well for us. The modern holy book *A Course in Miracles* suggests that Love is the solution. It describes that the ego—as a so-called 'player' or 'actor' (in our life's unfolding play)—is actually neither a player nor a person. Rather, the ego is a temporary and illusory kind of assistant or entity that we made, and which God did not make.

Why would we make the ego? *The Course* doesn't give a clear answer. Our personal guess is that we made the ego to help us sort and navigate as we journey on this divinely

Charles Whitfield and Barbara Whitfield

heard in your hello Oh, darlin', you're almost part of me Oh, darlin', you're all I'll ever see	mysterious adventure of our life on this planet and at times around unsafe people to help us survive.
The sound I have heard in your hello / Oh, darlin', you're all I'll ever see / Oh, darlin', you're almost part of me	This a beautiful and romantic poem-in-song that says something like "I not only love you, but I want to be with you for many reasons, including that The sound I have heard in your hello Oh, darlin', you're almost part of me Oh, darlin', you're all I'll ever see . We have here let go of our false self and begun to live real from our heart to help make a relationship work.

Legend of a Mind To most fans it is unforgettable. Most count it in their MB's top ten. Long and often performed in their concerts, it has not been done live since Ray retired from the band in 2002.

Ray wrote this captivating song well before they had finished *DoFP*. On the *Lost Chord* sleeve notes he said. "I'd heard through the grapevine about Timothy Leary and the Haight Ashbury scene, so I wrote these tongue-in-cheek lyrics. I saw the astral plane as a gaily-painted biplane where you paid a couple of bucks and they took you for a trip around the bay! When I met Tim Leary he knew that. He thought it was a hoot! ... People were coming up to us and saying, what's all this acid about? And we'd never seen acid. I'd read Tim Leary's psychedelic prayers in a couple of the books he'd written. The lyric "Timothy Leary's Dead" was just a reference to the *Tibetan Book of the Dead*."

162

Ray told us that he did not write it for any special spiritual reasons. [77] At the same time, as poetry critics acknowledge, there may be a few underlying dynamics that are worthwhile to explore.

Table A.7. Making Meaning of Legend of a Mind
by Ray Thomas from *ISoaLC* 1968

Lyrics	Our Suggested Meaning
Legend of a Mind Timothy Leary's dead / No, no, no He's outside looking in Repeat S-1	If any meaning could be made of these words, what would it be? We mentioned the *Tibetan Book of the Dead* and how it frames some of the psychedelic experience. [37]
He'll fly his astral plane Takes you trips around the bay / Brings you back the same day Timothy Leary x 2 Repeat S-1 x 2 Repeat S-2 Along the coast you'll hear them boast About a light they say that shines so clear So raise your glass, we'll drink a toast / To the little man / Who sells you thrills along the pier	Of course '…his astral plane' and 'back the same day' describe some of the effects of psychedelics, as do the later lyrics 'take you up, … bring you down / He'll plant your feet back firmly on the ground / He flies so high, he swoops so low' —except that after having a positive experience most have their values and how they see others and the world changed, and usually for the better. The 'light they say that shines so clear' is encountered in many other spiritual experiences, from NDEs to doing regular meditation to any of the other triggers we list on page 46 in Chapter 8. The rest of these lyrics reflect a poetic and musical tribute to both psychedelics and Leary.

He'll take you up, he'll bring you down / He'll plant your feet back firmly on the ground He flies so high, he swoops so low / He knows exactly which way he's gonna go Timothy Leary x 2 Repeat S-4 Repeat S-2	Another well placed song-within-a-song comes here 'Along the coast you'll hear them boast / About a light they say that shines so clear.' When the words stop for a while, the following longish instrumental with Ray's masterfully melodious flute and Mike's top Mellotron is one of the most naturally 'trippy' we have heard in all of music.

A few years later Mike wrote another tribute to Leary without naming him directly in 'When You're a Free Man' as the 7th of the 8 tracks in *Seventh Sojourn,* released in October 1972. That song is the *only* Moodies one that *mentions* the word *God*: Let's be **God**'s children / And live in perfect peace. Yet, as we show throughout this book, they composed, released and performed many glorious spiritual compositions over almost the last five decades.

After their early and long closeness as co-founders and band mates from 1964 to '72 Mike and Ray had a few years' hiatus. In 1978 they reunited briefly for *Octave* and remained mostly apart until the last few years and in 2011 they celebrated their 70th birthday together (see their picture taken together at that pivotal sentimental time online at mikepinder.com/?p=385#comments). They remain good friends to this day.

Fan and Reviewer Websites, incomplete list; there are likely several more we do not list here.

moodybluestoday.com "The official Moody Blues fan community." Tour and other most current info updates.

Kings of Classic Rock ref site: webwriter.f2s.com Devoted to the literal words of MBs, includes lyrics (incl. solo and miscellaneous recordings), their song books, commercial videos, and tour information from 1964-2011.

John McFerrin Music Reviews: Melody and Harmony johnmcferrinmusicreviews.org/mb.html

George Starotsin's Music Reviews, called 'Only Solitaire' found online at: starling.rinet.ru/music/moody.htm#Octave Be prepared for some controversy

Mark's (Prindle) reviews markprindle.com/moodya.htm

Prog Archives progarchives.com

Don Ignacio donignacio.com/music/moodybluespage.html

Ken's Links tstonramp.com/~macleod/banners.htm

MBs Fan Anthology at virtualtenkiller.com/moodyblues John Lodge is so right in saying that we all carry that Spirit.

FAQs on The Moody Blues otten.freeshell.org/moodyblues/FAQ-TOC.htm

Our Moodies website → **for your feedback** MoodiesBook.wordpress.com

REFERENCES

1 Adams D (2007) *Hitchhiker's Guide to the Galaxy*, Random House, NY

2 Altham K (Keith Altham was the most successful independent rock agent in the world from the early 70s to his retirement in 1993).

3 Archetypes en.wikipedia.org/wiki/Archetype Retrieved 20 Jan 2013

4 Beard D (2012) Revisit The Moody Blues' landmark album *Days of Future Passed.* goldminemag.com/article/revisit-the-moody-blues-landmark-album-days-of-future-passed

5 Benward B, Saker M (2003) *Music*: In Theory and Practice, Vol. I, Seventh Edition, McGraw-Hill

6 Bernhart K, Tuckosh K (Spring/Winter 1988) The making of the Mellotron. *Higher & Higher: The Moody Blues Magazine* p. 12-16 Geneva, Fl

7 Brown T themoodyblues.co.uk accessed Nov 2012

8 Brum Beat Links: brumbeat.net/bblinks.htm accessed Sept 2012

9 Childs MS, March J (2012) *Where Have All the Pop Stars Gone?* - Volume 2. EditPros, Davis, CA

10 Christgau R, Fricke D (12 July 2007). The 40 Essential Albums of 1967" *Rolling Stone* (Jann S Wenner). Retrieved 2012-07-30 robertchristgau.com/xg/rs/albums1967-07.php

11 Cohen GD (2005) *The Mature Mind*: The positive power of the aging brain. Basic Books, NY

12 Csíkszentmihalyi M (1990), *Flow:* The Psychology of Optimal Experience, New York: Harper and Row

13 DiGiacomo R (2012) John Lodge Interview: Moody Blues hit Caesars. 26 Nov, Atlantic City Insiders

14 Dilworth D (2009) a Superb Mellotron documentary for serious fans rhizome.org/editorial/2009/feb/11/interview-with-mellotron-documentary-filmmaker-dia   also see bazillionpoints.com/mellodrama/contact.html

15 Discography of Moody Blues
en.wikipedia.org/wiki/The_Moody_Blues_discography

16 Dow A, Dow S (accessed 12 Jan 2013) Describe their reactions runstop.de/moodies/about.html

17 Eder B (1967) Review of DoFP allmusic.com/album/r13367. Retrieved 3 Jan, 2013

18 Eder B (1997) Review of AQoB allmusic.com/album/a-question-of-balance-mw0000046519

19 Eder B (1969) Review of OtToaD allmusic.com/album/on-the-threshold-of-a-dream-mw0000626725

20 Eder B (1972) Review of SS. Bruce Eder is among their most attentive and prolific critics and archivists allmusic.com/album/seventh-sojourn mw0000191080

21 Edge G (2011) *The Written Works of Graeme Edge.* moodybluestoday.com/index.cfm/pk/view/cd/NAA/cdid/494155 /pid/400262 G

22 FAQs on Moody Blues otten.freeshell.org/moodyblues/FAQ-TOC.htm Superb and detailed information on them.

23 Frame P (2011) *Even More Rock Family Trees.* Omnibus Press

24 Gillabel D (2012) The Seven Shamanic Levels of Consciousness soul-guidance.com/houseofthesun/sevenlevels.htm ass. 7 Sept

25 Greenberg R (2010) Understanding the Fundamentals of Music. The Teaching Company

26 goldminemag.com/article/revisit-the-moody-blues-landmark-album-days-of-future-passed

27 Goswami A (2011) *How Quantum Activism Can Save Civilization.* Hampton Books, Charlottesville, VA

28 Hameroff S, Penrose R Near-Death Experiences Explained by Quantum Physicists quantumconsciousness.org/ (2013)

29 Harrison E (2008) Time warp. *Cosmos,* Issue 20, April cosmosmagazine.com/node/2187/full

30 Herman J (1992) *Trauma and Recovery.* BasicBooks, N Y

31 Hermes W (January 2004). Essential Prog Rock. *Spin* (Vibe/Spin Ventures) **20** (1): 48. Retrieved 2012-07-29 books.google.com/books?id=6CTUGqnYjTwC&pg=PA48#v=one page&q&f=false.

32 Holdship B The Moody Blues Reviews. Yahoo Music. Arch from the original on 2012-07-29. Retrieved 2012-07-29 http://music.ca.launch.yahoo.com/read/review/12031589

33 James G (about 1996) accessed 2 Jan 2013 Interview with Mike Pinder at classicbands.com/MikePinderInterview.html

34 Jimmy Durante (1947) "I'm the guy who found the Lost Chord" imdb.com/name/nm0002051/

35 Journal Troubadour en.wikipedia.org/wiki/Folk_music (Troubadours)

36 Krippner S (2011) Altered and transitional states [of consciousness]. In MA Runco & SR Pritzker (eds), *Encyclopedia of Creativity*, 2nd ed vol 1, pp 33-39 San Diego, CA: Academic Press

37 Leary, T (accessed 27 Dec 2012) en.wikipedia.org/wiki/Timothy_Leary Also en.wikipedia.org/wiki/Legend_of_a_Mind

38 Lerner M (2009) The Moody Blues *Threshold of a Dream* Live at the Isle of Wight Festival, Pulsar Productions, Eagle Rock Entertainment . Recommended viewing for all fans and friends.

39 Littlefield C (2002) *Hofmann's Potion.* Yo Tube *
yoism.org/?q=node/52#   (Scroll down about half way here)

40 Lodge J (1972) Isn't life strange. Lyrics by author and sung by
The Moody Blues. en.wikipedia.org/wiki/Isn%27t_Life_Strange
and www.youtube.com/watch?v=9WZZjXgJ4W8&feature=results_
main&playnext=1&list=PL2D0013FF6A366A69

41 LSD mystical refs
theuniversesolved.com/theuniversesolved/yetanotherforum/yaf_p
ostst655_Moody-Blues-as-soulmanifesting-music.aspx

42 Lying en.wikipedia.org/wiki/Lie#Barefaced_lie

43 Lyrics sources (accessed 5 Jan 2013) most are in public domain
e.g.,:azlyrics.com/m/moody.html
lyricsfreak.com/m/moody+blues/   —widely   available   on
Internet

44 Mark's (Prindle) reviews markprindle.com/moodya.htm

45 Marshall G (2102) Postcards from a Rock & Roll Tour.
foreword by Graeme Edge, Splendid Books, UK
splendidbooks.co.uk/books/postcards-from-a-rock-roll-tour/

46 McFerrin J Reviews at johnmcferrinmusicreviews.org/mb.html

47 Mellotron sound on YouTube assembled by charel196's channel
'The Mellotronic Symphony.' A *superb remix* of some of the best
from Mellotron master Mike Pinder, original Moody Blues co-
founder and keyboardist, compiled into a symphonic stream-of-
consciousness, and found online on (25 Jan 2013)
youtube.com/watch?v=jpLaCSVR_0o

48 Mendelsohn J (original Nov 12, 1970) Review of AQoB. *Rolling
Stone* magazine.   superseventies.com/spmoodies1.html

49 MeridCEO@AOL.COM (1999) amazon.com/gp/cdp/member-
reviews/A1DOZUAFDZWLLZ/ref=cm_cr_pr_auth_rev?ie=UTF8&sor
t_by=MostRecentReview

50 Moerman M (1984) Interview with Justin *Higher & Higher: The
Moody Blues Magazine,* Geneva, Fl

51 Moerman M (1984) Mike Pinder: One step into the light. Parts 1 and 2, *Higher & Higher: The Moody Blues Magazine,* Geneva, Fl Fall/Winter

52 Moodies' FAQ list: otten.freeshell.org/moodyblues/FAQ-TOC.htm

53 Moody Blues **Fan sites**: Do a simple web search for 'moody blues fan site' – some are not active

54 Moody Blues home page online: moodybluestoday.com/

55 Murley M, Salas R, Murley T (1983-1992) *Higher & Higher: The Moody Blues Magazine* Geneva, Fl

56 Parapsychology (accessed 3 Jan 2013) en.wikipedia.org/wiki/Parapsychology

57 Piirto J (2011) Poetry. in Runco MA, Pritzker SR (eds) *Encyclopedia of Creativity* vol 2, 2nd ed 244-9

58 Piirto J (2011) Synchronicity and creativity. in Runco MA, Pritzker SR (eds) *Encyclopedia of Creativity* vol 2, 2nd ed 409-13

59 Pinder M (2013) Personal communications, 1 Feb-1 March

60 Poetry - Key ref faculty.gvsu.edu/websterm/Readpoem.htm

61 Powell M (2006) sleeve text update for OtToaD, SACD version

62 Price J (1990) The Justin Hayward interview. *Higher & Higher: The Moody Blues Magazine* Geneva, Fl, Winter

63 Progressive/ProgRock archives & music term definitions at progarchives.com/artist.asp?id=224

64 Psychedelics research (accessed 12 Jan 2013) small fee charged for each informative paper at spiritualcompetency.com described by many of the original authors

65 Putney K (1985) A conversation with Justin Hayward. *Higher & Higher: The Moody Blues Magazine* Geneva, Fl, Fall/Winter p 9-18

66 Rock *Family Trees* by Pete Frame blog.familyofrock.com

67 Root-Bernstein R, & M (2011) Life stages of creativity. in Runco MA, Pritzker SR (eds) *Encyclopedia of Creativity* vol 2, 2nd ed 47-55

68 Say what you mean article in psychologytoday.com/blog/life-saving-philosophy/201002/do-you-say-what-you-mean and book by Runion M (2010) *Speak Strong*: Say what you mean. Mean what you say. Don't be mean when you say it. Morgan James Publishing

69 Sammy Sultan interviews Justin Hayward huffingtonpost.co.uk/sammy-sultan/interview-with-justin-hayward-of-the-moody-blues_b_2658429.html

70 Sciaky E (1990) The Moody Blues Story. Band members' radio interviews and music, on CD, February, Philadelphia, PA

71 Sound On Sound (Classic Tracks: The Moody Blues Nights in White Satin") by Richard Buskin Retrieved 25 Jan 2013 soundonsound.com/sos/jul09/articles/classictracks_0709.htm

72 sing365.com/music/lyric.nsf/Graeme-Edge-Biography/AD7A71522248FDCA48256A6A002D1C11

73 Starotsin's, George, Music Reviews, called 'Only Solitaire' found online at: starling.rinet.ru/music/moody.htm#Octave

74 Tart C on Consciousness and altered states. psychedelic-library.org/soc2.htm (accessed 27 Jan 2013)

75 Texture, musical en.wikipedia.org/wiki/Musical_texture

76 The Moody Blues : "The Kings of Classic Rock website webwriter.f2s.com/ ...Lyrics and more

77 Thomas, Ray (2013) Personal communications, 1 Feb- March

78 Time references en.wikipedia.org/wiki/Time

79 TOCCC cduniverse.com/productinfo.asp?pid=%208717068

80 Tracy J, Shinder S (1996) *Time Traveler*. Moody Blues Boxed Two sets of 4 and 5 CDs available, Polydor/Threshold

81 Treasure trove of articles and information on Moodies : moodybluesattitude.yuku.com/topic/278/Online-articles-Master-List-1003-articles-with-hot-links

82 Values Sources Pavlina S (2013) Living Your Values. stevepavlina.com/articles/living-your-values-1.htm and stevepavlina.com
Abbot H (213) helenabbott.com/resources/core-values-list

83 Wendt JA Hymms To The Consciousness Soul: An Imagined Philosophy of the Moody Blues. Assesed Sept 2012 ipwebdev.com/hermit/aipmb.html

84 webwriter.f2s.com/wings/moodies.htm   more on MBs

85 Weil AT (2011) *Spontaneous Happiness*

86 Whitfield B 1995. *Spiritual Awakenings: Insights of the Near-Death Experience and other Doorways to our Soul.* Health Communications, Inc. Deerfield Beach, FL

87 Whitfield CL: *Healing the Child Within*: Discovery & recovery for adult children of dysfunctional families. Health Communications, Deerfield Beach, FL, 1987 ... also translated and published in French, German, Spanish, Portuguese, Italian, Farsi, Japanese, Croatian, Arabic and Korean

88 Whitfield CL: *Choosing God*: A Bird's Eye View of *A Course in Miracles.* Muse House press, Atlanta 2010

89 Whitfield CL: *Teachers of God*: Further Reflections on *A Course in Miracles.* Muse House press, Atlanta 2010

90 Whitfield CL: *Wisdom to Know the Difference*: Core Issues in Relationships, Recovery and Living. Muse House Press, Atlanta, Ga 2012

91 Whitfield CL (2011) *Not Crazy:* You May Not Be Mentally Ill - Misdiagnosed and mistreated with drugs that don't work well or make you worse. Muse House Press, Atlanta, Ga

92 Wincentsen E (2001) *The Moody Blues Companion* Wynn Publishing, Pickens, SC

93 wiki.answers.com/Q/What_makes_poetry_different_to_other_forms_of_writing#ixzz28AesS78t

94 Whitfield CL Whitfield BH (2014) *Engaging the Muse: Creativity in:* the arts, the professions, relationships, health and living, literature, business, management, economics, architecture, design–industrial & graphic, advertising, mathematics, music, science, engineering, psychology, medicine, philosophy, history, politics, economics, entertainment, sports, and teaching. Muse House Press, Atlanta, GA

95 en.wikipedia.org/wiki/Mellotron

96 en.wikipedia.org/wiki/Timbre

97 Zimmerman L (accessed 4 Jan 2013) John Lodge Interview on *DoFP.* goldminemag.com/article/moody-blues-bassist-john-lodge-looks-back-on-days-of-future-passed

98 MBs photos: This photo file is licensed under the Creative Commons Attribution Share Alike 3.0 Netherlands license.

100 Lousararian, L (2013) Personal communications, Rogers and Cowan, Los Angeles, by mail, phone and e-mails, Jan-Feb

* For ref **39** above, this is a documentary that shows a more balanced look at LSD and how it fits into our world. Long before Leary the drug was studied as a way to treat forms of addiction and mental illness. It was being found as a strong tool for mental exploration and self-understanding. With interviews with LSD research pioneers, beautiful music and stunning cinematography, this is another way of looking at the drug and our world.

INDEX

More from Muse House Press

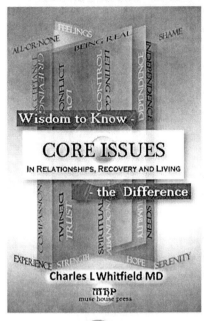

This book addresses in detail these common Core Issues in Relationships Recovery and Living.

» Needing to be in control
» Difficulty trusting
» Difficulty being real
» How to handle feelings
» Low self-esteem (shame)
» Dependence & Independence
» Fear of abandonment
» All-or-non thinking
» High Tolerance for Inappropriate Behavior
» Over-responsibility for others
» Neglecting my own needs
» Grieving my ungrieved losses
» Difficulty resolving conflict
» Difficulty giving/receiving love

"In my over 30 years assisting countless people with a variety of mental, emotional, behavior. and relationship problems, I have come to realize that many of them have been misdiagnose and mistreated. In fact, most o them were not mentally ill. In this book I share research and experience and offer hope and another way that may success-fully address what may not be a "mental illness"

—Charles Whitfield MD

More from Muse House Press

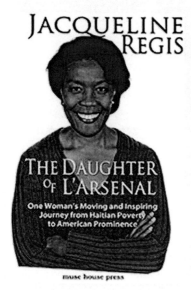

JACQUELINE REGIS

THE DAUGHTER OF L'ARSENAL

One Woman's Moving and Inspiring Journey from Haitian Poverty to American Prominence

muse house press

A inspiring story of a woman of two worlds. In this moving memoir of love and driven determination against all odds, Jacqueline Regis, an accomplished lawyer and judge, tells the story of her climb up from poverty in Haiti to prominence in America in vivid and stirring detail. She shares with us the hope and inspiration to keep reaching higher for our goals, and never giving in to anything less.

This book will inspire you to make the most of your life!

"...many tools and techniques to help the reader transform the ordinary difficulties of life into moments of calm, clarity and, sometimes, surprisingly, even the deepest joy. And they do it not only skillfully but with humor, too. This is a book to treasure --and to keep handy."

Kenneth Ring, PhD
Author of
Lessons from the Light

A Guide to Self-Awareness and Change

BARBARA HARRIS WHITFIELD AND SHARON K. CORMIER
Foreword by Charles L. Whitfield, MD

CPSIA information can be obtained at www.ICGtesting.com
Printed in the USA
LVOW08s1214010913

350469LV00002B/606/P

9 781935 827153